SWIM FOR LIFE

To Susan —
Hope you keep
enjoying Swimming —
Love,
Bobbie

Books by Barbara Callison

Humphrey The Whale Who Lost His Way   1987

Growing Up In Los Altos   1992

SWIM FOR LIFE

DR. BARBARA CALLISON

Barcal Press

Los Altos

For information about permission to reproduce selections
from this book, write to the author at
450 San Luis Avenue
Los Altos, California, 94024

Printed in the United States of America

ISBN 0-9665297-0-7

Cover Design by The Visual Group, Palo Alto

Graphic Production by Topping House Ltd., Palo Alto

Book Design by Jack Halliday

Cover Photos of: Adam Peterson, diver; Maleah Callison, preschool swimmer;
Kristina Lum and Bill May, Santa Clara Aquamaids Synchronized Swimming;
Angela Romano, age-group swimmer; Aldo Da Rosa, Master Swimmer

Dedication

This book is dedicated
to my grandchildren
Stephanie, Laura, Michael,
Michelle, Jason, Maleah,
Morgan and Steven.
I hope they enjoy the water as much as I have.

Acknowledgments

I could not have written this book
without the support of my fellow swimmers.
I appreciate the time given
by all the swimmers and coaches
who shared information with me during interviews.
I am especially indebted to Rinconada Masters swimmers
Dick Bennett, Aldo Da Rosa, Ann Kay, Judith Schwartz and Eloise Danto
for their input, guidance, and editing.

Thank you, Norm Manoogian for your advice
over the years on weight training.
And, thanks to Mo Chambers who suggested the title.

And last but certainly not least, many thanks
to Jack Halliday who encouraged me to publish
and offered technical advice.

Table of Contents

This book illustrates the "whys and ways" to incorporate swimming into a lifelong physical fitness program. In order to perform physical activity, one should have a working knowledge of nutrition, and know what to expect as one ages. Physical fitness is a lifestyle. It includes not only physical but emotional and spiritual aspect of one's life.

The 1996 Olympics brought swimming to the public eye as record-breaking performances were watched by millions of people throughout the world. Beauty, coordination and well-conditioned muscles were the trademarks of swimmers who participated in synchronized, diving and swim competition events. The Olympic swimmer is aging. For the first time, two Master swimmers (over age 24) earned medals in Olympic events. Older swimmers also earned medals in diving.

Anyone age 21 or older who has a working knowledge of the four basic swim strokes—free, back, breast and fly can join a Masters swim program for a nominal fee. Physical fitness is the primary goal of Master programs.

There is no other sport that leaves one feeling as refreshed and relaxed as swimming, even after a difficult training session. Where else can a human being begin life in a water environment in the womb and stay in a water environment until departure from this life? Swimming is a lifelong sport that enhances not only the body but the mind as well.

Swimming is intergenerational. There are families of children, parents and grandparents all participating together in swim programs and competition events. The phrase, "it takes a community to raise a child", applies to swim activities.

Swimming is the most popular sport in the United States but it is also the least publicized sport. It is estimated that over 200 million boys, girls and adults participate in some form of swimming in the United States. Swimming is not a professional sport which most likely accounts for the lack of publicity.

In recent years, there has been a decline in the number of US age-group swimmers on swim teams. Age-group swimmers may start as young as five years and continue through eighteen years of age. This decrease has been offset by a growing increase in the number of adults on Masters swim teams. This change can be explained by several factors. Today both boys and girls have more options and competition for their free time than they did 15 years ago. Energy costs for heating water have increased over the years, raising the fee for swim team membership. On the other hand, older adults are more health oriented today, realizing the value of exercise as a part of their daily lives. Many Master teams offer discounts for Senior citizens. Master swimming provides an opportunity for young and older adults to work and socialize together. Masters swimming in the US has reached 33,000 registered members with new clubs being formed daily.

A section of this book is dedicated to the number one growing sport in the United States, Masters swimming. What type of person is drawn to Masters swimming? You may be surprised to learn that most of these swimmers are noncompetitors and come from a background with a love of the water but not necessarily professional training. Tips and training routines of interviewed swimmers that belong to swim clubs across the United States are summarized. There are many reasons why Masters swimmers are interesting, energetic and optimistic.

Other sections of the book impart information about the different ways swimming can become a part of your life. A working knowledge of stroke mechanics, muscle and cardiovascular physiology and energy

requirements is included to enable swimmers to increase performance rates and interest in the sport.

Discussions with fellow swimmers have centered around ways to age gracefully but efficiently. Since everyone will get older, there is a section on the mechanics of aging and ways to test biological age. Aging is a complicated process. I tried to solve this problem by supplying a simplified version as well as a more complicated version for the avid reader.

I have a love and respect for the water. I grew up swimming for fun. Later I taught water safety courses and swim instruction at all age levels. But, Masters swimming has been the most positive force in my life. I started Master workouts at age forty with no previous competitive training. I marvel at the human body's response to an exercise program, both physically and mentally. With the proper instruction, practice and motivation, stroke efficiency and physical fitness can be achieved at any age. The best part is having fun while achieving these goals. The second best part is personal observation how swimming has helped people deal with the ups and downs of daily life.

The book is divided into topical sections. Each section or chapter can be read independently of the previous chapter. If all you want to know is about aging, you can turn to Chapter 13 and feel assured that all the information needed is there in the one chapter. My hope is that I can share with you my love for the water and help you find a place in the swimming world where you can have fun and feel comfortably challenged. Finding your niche in a sport is important to lifelong participation. Swimming offers many options.

Not every one needs to be a world class swimmer. As a Masters swimmer I feel privileged to have shared the starting blocks with Olympics greats such as Shane Gould, Ann Curtis, and Gail Roper. In 1996 at the De Anza Masters Short Course Championships, I watched Aileen Soule, the oldest Olympic swimmer, compete at age 90. Her stroke mechanics were good and she set a new record in the 50 yard freestyle by 38 seconds. She was slim with excellent posture and a good conversationalist. That is the way I want to be at age 90! I know swimming will help me get there.

Three Generations of Swimmers in the Baxter Family

The Baxter Family. Rear: Tristin Baxter, Mitchell Ryan. Middle row: (l–r) Steve, Olympic contender in Fly; Erin Reiland, Jr. National swimmer; Kyle Baxter, An Simmons Baxter, Olympic Gold Medalist in Freestyle; Jo Jo Baxter, National Age-Group recordholder; Trent Baxter, Kathy Baxter, Terri Baxter Smith, Olympic contender in Breaststroke. Front: Cindy Baxter, Coach, Rinconada Masters Swim Team.

Why Should I Swim?

1

Swimming is the number one participant sport in the United States. Approximately 200 million children and adults participate in one of many swim activities. It is gaining in popularity. Does this information surprise you as you pick up a newspaper and read about tennis, soccer, baseball and so on but not swimming events? The best reason for the low profile is lack of professional teams, thus little publicity.

Swimming has many advantages over other sports. To start with, age does not matter. It is an intergenerational sport. Families can swim together. Swimming may start before walking and continue until 70, 80 or a 100 years of age. In fact, the oldest registered Masters swimmer is Tom Lane at age 101. He competed in the 1996 United States Short Course Championships held in California. Age may slow swimming times but stroke efficiency remains intact. The youngest swimmer I have taught was 6 months old.

Swimming is not a seasonal sport. Pools, lakes, rivers and the ocean provide individuals with the opportunity to swim year-round. In the west and southwestern United States, swimming is generally all year round in outdoor pools. In the middle and eastern states, indoor pools are available. The hardy swimmer, better known as a "polar bear" celebrates the New Year with January swims in waters that range from 30 to 50 degrees. A few popular areas for polar bears swims are San Francisco Bay, Chicago lakefront, Milwaukee, Sheboygan, Wisconsin, Boulder, Colorado, and Newport, Rhode Island.

Unlike other sports, swimming takes on many forms that are open to males and females equally. The water is not a natural medium for humans. How to take a breath without inhaling water, and how to move without expending a lot of energy are important skills to learn. Therefore, swim lessons are a part of many children's summer experiences.

Several types of water activities are discussed in the next few paragraphs. A more detailed version of some of the sports is included in Chapter 3.

Recreational swimming is the most popular

, just having fun in the water. It can be done in a pool, ocean, river or lake. Swimming in the summer at the beach or a favorite lake is a cherished childhood memory for many adults. These same adults may choose to swim in a lap program at a pool as part of a physical conditioning regime.

Water exercise classes are another option. They are designed to be motivational and fun while increasing muscle flexibility and strength. The water provides resistance, making it a useful medium to develop muscle tone. Two advantages to this form of activity are the head never has to go in the water and swimming skills are not a requirement. Combinations of arm and kick drills with aerobic-type exercises keep joints flexible. For many years, women were the only participants in water exercise but lately I have seen a few men.

Individuals with a talent for the water have many opportunities to use swimming skills. If you like competition and want to improve your swim technique, join a swim team. Swim teams accommodate all age groups. Competitive events are judged in two year increments, starting at age six to age eighteen. Some places even have a category for six and unders. It is important to check out the program and coaching technique for young children to prevent "burn out" in later years. Make sure the children are having fun. If they are, they probably won't realize the amount of skills being acquired and will want to stay connected with a swim program.

Most high schools and colleges offer swim programs. One of the fastest growing sports in high school, especially among girls, is water polo. It is an outlet for swimmers to participate in a team sport, using their swimming abilities. A knowledge of game rules, plus speed stamina is required. Girls who never swam on a swim team are attracted to water polo as a new sport to try. These girls previously participated in other team sports such as volleyball or baseball.

Master swim teams begin at age nineteen with competitive events judged in five year increments. The four competitive strokes are freestyle, backstroke, breaststroke and butterfly. Shallow dives and efficient turns are part of the learning process.

If heights and gymnastics moves are preferred, try a diving team. Diving is a solo performance that is judged for its accuracy, grace and beauty. If you prefer to work in small groups and like the grace and beauty of ballet, try synchronized swimming. The routines are performed to music. Many of the moves are under the water which requires good breath control.

For those individuals who have endurance and do not wish to be confined to a pool environment, there is distance swimming in lakes or the ocean. You must be able to tolerate colder water, fish, seaweed, and sometimes waves. The distances can vary from one mile to five miles. An advantage is enjoying the scenery while swimming. These events have become increasingly popular with adult swimmers. Some places even offer children's distances along with the adults to encourage family participation. Or family relays are a great way to provide friendly competition in distance swimming.

Swimming is not expensive compared to other sports. Think of the equipment cost and fees to go skiing or play golf. Compare these costs with what swimming requires. You need a source of water—pool, lake, river or ocean. Equipment includes a bathing suit which is generally made of lycra and nylon. Female suits are more expensive than male suits, presumably because there is more material involved. You can increase the wearing length of a bathing suit with careful attention to a few pointers. To prevent damage to lycra fibers by chemicals in the water, rinse suits in cold water after each wearing. If new suits are purchased and not worn immediately, store them in the freezer to maintain elasticity of nylon and lycra fibers. Last year's models can be obtained at a discounted price through swim catalogs or in special bins at sport stores. The suit should be snug enough to prevent air and water from lying against the body. Many swimmers continue to wear worn-out suits over a new suit to create drag. Worn-out suits stretch and allow water and air to enter the space between the new and old suit, creating friction or drag. The swimmer must work harder in the water to counter the effects of friction. When the drag suit is removed, the swimmer speeds through the water!

Many individuals purchase goggles to protect the eyes from chemicals in the water. There is a wide variety of styles and sizes but most goggles are between five and ten dollars and last for several swim seasons.

They should also be rinsed in cold water to remove chemical residues. It is important to find a style that fits your eye socket to prevent water leakage. Also, a small percentage of individuals are allergic to plastic in the goggle liner. There are foam-based liners. Therefore, try on several styles before making a purchase.

A bathing cap keeps long hair secure and protects hair from the damaging effects of the sun's rays and chlorine. Bathing caps reduce the amount of water entering the ears. Again, there is a wide choice of sizes and styles. Latex and nylon caps last the longest but cost a few dollars more. Most caps are under five dollars. Rinse caps in cold water after each use, and apply talc powder to rubber caps to lessen sticking and tearing.

Fins, paddles and buoys are optional equipment that may enhance stroke technique. Most sport stores carry a wide variety of styles and the cost varies with each style. The shorter, "Zoomer" fins are better for the more advanced swimmers as they force the swimmer to work harder. The longer the fin, the easier the leg action. Long fins are a good way to correct flaws in the kicking motion. Resist the temptation to become dependent on fins to cover more distance. Different style paddles are designed for specific stroke action. It is advisable to have instruction from a coach before using paddles. Injury to shoulder joints is possible, particularly if the wrong size or style is used. Buoys are styrofoam floats placed between the legs that change body position and limit leg action. They are used to encourage arm pulling only. If body position is not streamlined, "meaning hips tend to sink below water surface", buoys will raise the hips. Use buoys to get a feel for where the hips and legs should be but resist using them on a permanent basis.

The biggest advantage to swimming is the role it plays in physical fitness. Improvement in overall health occurs at all age levels. It is the best sport for cardiovascular fitness. Asthmatics find improvement in breathing with regular swim workouts. The best known swimming asthmatics are Nancy Hogshead who won medals in the 1984 Olympics and Tom Dolan who medaled in the 1996 Olympics in Atlanta. Details of improvement to the respiratory system are described in Chapter 13.

Swimming is a great stress reducer. It is relaxing and relieves muscle tension. Swimming horizontal in the water takes pressure off the back and legs. It also strengthens back, shoulder and leg muscles. A swimming break during the work day allows individuals to perform more efficiently the rest of the day.

Swimming is marvelous for healthy pregnant women. It increases circulation which benefits Mom and the growing fetus. It decreases pressure in leg veins which allows blood to circulate faster back to the heart. A horizontal position also relieves pressure on abdominal organs. Swimming increases muscle tone which benefits the labor phase. Water is a soothing medium that promotes relaxation. A bonus—it is a great stress reducer to continue after the baby arrives!

Swimming is excellent for children with disabilities. Children who lack coordination benefit from the "patterning" motion of swimming skills. Since all body extremities are used, nerve pathways are stimulated which improves balance and coordination. Swimming is the one sport where blind children have the freedom to exercise muscles without fear of injury. They learn to count strokes to determine the end of the pool. I have taught children with one arm or one leg to swim—just modify the arm or leg movement to compensate for the imbalance.

A big plus is that swimming has the fewest injuries of any sport. The water is a wonderful shock absorber. Swimming maintains muscle strength without placing undue stress on muscles, tendons, ligaments and joints. Occasionally, a swimmer may develop shoulder injuries from overtraining or incorrect use of paddles. Good coaching results in few injuries. On the other side of the coin, swimming is recommended by doctors as a form of physical therapy to recuperate from knee surgery, hip replacement and arthritic conditions.

Swimming builds beautiful bodies at any age. It uses the most muscle groups of any sport. Swimming tones the entire body. Both upper and lower body muscles are needed for stroke competition, diving, synchro and water polo.

Swimming lengthens muscles, giving a long, lean appearance to the body. Teenagers who swim regularly worry less about dieting than their nonathletic friends. It is best to start at an early age for maximum benefits but older adults profit by increasing the ratio of muscle to fat tissue in the body.

After all of the above advantages, one reason remains. The water makes you feel good. Other sports leave you hot and sweaty after a workout, while swimming leaves you feeling cool, refreshed and relaxed.

Oldies But Goodies

Mary Jane Reeves (81), Sally Joy (81), Jae Howell (76), Jean Durston (84). Walnut Creek Masters. 800 Free Relay Record Holders at Pacific Masters Short Course Championships, Santa Clara, 1998.

Mother and Daughter

Carol Macpherson and Ellen Tait

San Mateo Marlins

l to r. Helen Roumasset, Audrey Etienne, Zada Taft, Ray Taft

A Tour Through Swimming History

2

Swimming has been around for a very long time! It predates the time before Christ was born. Historians agree from evidence found in cave drawings that many ancient cultures swam, using the "dog paddle" or modified freestyle stroke. They probably first swam because they needed to cross a body of water and watched animals swim successfully. Drawings indicate the Egyptians and Greeks were swimming as early as 2100 BC.

Through the ages, swimming styles, techniques and attire have changed dramatically as new technology emerged. Today, interest in swimming is facilitated by cyberspace with the access of e-mail and the Internet. Places to swim, workouts, and where to buy swim gear are located on Internet web pages.

Swimming began out of necessity then emerged into pleasure. Competition came later. Around 36 BC, organized swimming was introduced in both Japan and Rome. Japan had simple races and the Romans introduced the first heated pools. Romans enjoyed the therapeutic benefits of warm water. Our present culture has modified this idea into spas and hot tubs. It wasn't until the 17th century that Japan introduced compulsory, organized swimming into their educational system.

One of the first known books about the sport appeared in 1538, titled, "The Art of Swimming". But, swimming did not increase steadily in popularity. The number of people swimming declined during the epidemics of the Middle Ages. People thought disease was spread by means of water. During the 1940's as polio cases reached epidemic proportions, people stayed away from the water for the same reason. Today it is known that swimming does not transmit disease any more readily than any other activities.

Even though the Japanese included swimming as a form of exercise in the early 17th century, the rest of the world did not actively start to swim until the mid 1800's. England was the first country to spread the popularity of swimming for recreation and as a competitive sport.

In 1837, six indoor pools opened in London

with most people swimming for recreation. The popular strokes at this time all kept the head out of the water and the arms recovered under water. Breaststroke was swum using a frog-like kick. The side stroke was performed with the swimmer lying on his or her side in the water. A scissors-like kick propelled this stroke. The "dog paddle" which was similar to present-day freestyle used a modified flutter kick.

It was not until 1873 that the first over-the-water alternating arm recovery was introduced. John Trudgen of London observed natives in South America using this type of a stroke. He perfected the motion and introduced it in London as a new stroke, called the trudgen. The arms looked like our present-day freestyle but the legs used a scissors kick. He proceeded to set a world record by swimming this stroke for 100 yards in 60 seconds. Not only could one swim faster but it was less tiring than other strokes. This new form promoted long - distance swimming which was the primary form of competition for many years.

Swimming as a sport continued to grow in England and across the world. England had many firsts in swimming. It was here that rudimentary water polo games were held in open water in the 1860's. The London Sporting Association included swimming as one of its programs in 1869. The first national swimming federation was formed in England in 1874. One year later, the first man, Captain Matthew Webb, swam across the English Channel.

Two other events increased the status of swimming. In the United States, competitive

swimming was organized with the formation of the Amateur Athletic Union (AAU) in 1888. This same organization today is called US Swimming (USS). The second major event was the inclusion of swimming in the modern Olympics held in Athens, Greece, 1896. At this time there were 3 races and only men were allowed to compete. Women's races were not added until 1912 in the Stockholm Olympics.

Australia had a claim to fame in the swimming arena with the advent of the "Australian crawl", a name associated with the freestyle stroke used today. A continuous 6 beat flutter kick replaced the scissors kick used previously with the trudgen stroke. Hawaiians and other islanders swam this stroke in the late 1800's. But, Australia received the credit in 1902 when Richard Cavill swam the 100 yard freestyle with a flutter kick in a new time of 58.6 seconds in a pool in Australia. A new record and a new stroke went into the history books!

Backstroke appeared in the early 1900's, swum on the back using an inverted breast stroke kick coordinated with a double arm pull and recovery. Today this elementary backstroke, as it is called, is used by recreational swimmers and some Master swimmers. Later, the racing backstroke evolved. The flutter kick replaced the breaststroke kick and alternating arms were used for pull and recovery phases. This is the only form allowed in competition today, excluding Master events.

Butterfly is another stroke that was initially developed using the breaststroke kick. The stroke is swum on the stomach, both arms pull underwater simultaneously accompanied by an overwater recovery. In 1953, butterfly became a separate official competitive stroke with a dolphin kick. As in the backstroke, Master swimmers are the only group allowed to compete using the breaststroke kick with butterfly arms.

The individual medley consisting of four consecutive strokes swum in the order of butterfly, backstroke, breaststroke and freestyle did not become an official event in the Olympics until 1964.

The United States has produced many powerful swimmers who set national and world records. Most of these swimmers participated in the Olympics. Only a few memorable individuals will be mentioned.

First on the scene was Duke Kahanamoku, an outstanding Hawaiian sprinter. Although he had no formal swim lessons, he won the 100 meter freestyle at the 1912 and 1920 Olympics. There were no Olympics in 1916 due to World War I.

In 1924, Johnny Weissmuller took over as the reigning freestyler at the Olympics. He repeated his performance again in 1928. Not only did he set fifty world records but he became the famous Tarzan of the movies. His contribution to the popularity of swimming is known mostly through his athletic endeavors in films.

Gertrude Ederle went down in the history books as the first woman to swim the English Channel in 1926, and the first woman to break the previous men's record. Although she had won national titles in the 400 and 800 meter freestyle, she became famous for her marathon swims.

Buster Crabbe followed Johnny Weissmuller as the champion freestyler in the late 1920's and early 1930's. He won gold medals in the 1932 Olympics. From there he went on to star in movies, television and swim promotions. He actively supported the inception of the Masters swim program in the early 1970's, and participated in the first championships. He swam with a Masters team until his death.

The 1940's brought a new decade of swimmers, ones that I remember as I learned to swim. Ann Curtis was and still is a superb freestyler, although tennis is her sport today. She swam briefly with a Masters team in the 1970's. She won many national freestyle titles in the 1940's, starting at age eleven and culminating with the 1948 Olympics in London. She earned medals in the 100 and 400 individual freestyle events plus the 400 meter relay. Her male counterpart at this time was Joe Verdeur, a fantastic breaststroker. He, too, won national titles in breaststroke and individual medley. In the London Olympics he took a gold in the 200 meter breaststroke.

A style of swimming called water ballet came to movie screens across the world in the 40's and 50's as MGM produced movies starring Esther Williams. She and Johnny Weissmuller performed together in the 1940 San Francisco World's Fair Aquacade. Esther could hold her breath forever while performing graceful moves in fantastic costumes and make-up. Later, synchronized swimming became popular as little girls wanted to look and swim like Esther Williams.

In the last forty years, United States swimmers and divers have remained at the forefront by setting national and world records. They have been challenged by the Germans, Japanese, Australians and Chinese. But access to pools and excellent affordable training programs allowed the US to maintain a depth of outstanding swimmers.

During the 60's and 70's, California produced outstanding talent. The following coaches had powerful teams during this period: George Haines, of the Santa Clara Swim Club, Sherm Chavoor of Arden Hills Swim Club in Sacramento, and Mark Schubert with Mission Viejo in Southern California. Who can forget Olympic swimmers such as Don Schollander, a versatile freestyler, who earned gold medals in distance events as well as sprints. A difficult feat to achieve! Or Debbie Meyer who won the 200, 400 and 800 meter freestyle events at the Mexico City Olympics in 1968.

Donna DeVarona from the Santa Clara Swim Club promoted swimming for women in many ways. First, she captured the 400 individual medley and a relay in the 1964 Tokyo games. Then she went to work for NBC as a female sportscaster for swim events in a male-dominated field. In 1975 she joined President Ford's Commission on Olympic Sports, and later campaigned for Title IX to give women equal representation in sports.

Great swimmers of the 1970's were Mark Spitz who entered the record books for being the first to set seven world records, accompanied by seven gold medals in the 1972 Olympics at Munich. Cynthia Woodhead

from Mission Viejo excelled in freestyle during this time period. Tall and lean, John Nabor set two world records in Montreal in the 100 and 200 meter backstroke.

Outstanding swimmers in the 1980's and 90's benefited from new training techniques and newer technology that made the body more streamlined and faster. The International Center for Swimming Research in Colorado Spring tests stroke mechanics, blood chemistry and muscle chemistry as swimmers perform in a submarine tank called a flume. Water is moved past the swimmer as he or she swims in place. Underwater videos impart to the coach and swimmer where minute changes in stroke technique benefit swimming times. Here swimming is being analyzed at the molecular cell level to determine how muscles could perform more efficiently. The Center is committed to research on human performance and education programs for athletes and coaches.

Tracy Caulkins emerged during this period with a new style of breaststroke that earned her gold medals at the Olympics. Her arms recovered over the top of the water to reduce drag and swim times. She has the distinction of being the only American swimmer ever to hold all of the US records at the same time. Quite an achievement!

During this same period, Mary T. Meagher reigned as "Madame Butterfly" for 15 years by setting world records, winning gold medals and losing few butterfly races.

Every four years, the scene changes with new, young swimmers joining the older veterans. The 1988 Olympics sported swimming greats Matt Biondi and youngster Janet Evans. Matt earned 7 gold medals while Janet at age 17 earned 3 gold medals and was on her way to being the greatest distance swimmer in the world. Since then she has participated in the 1992 and 1996 Olympics. She currently holds 3 world and 6 American records. Besides being a great distance swimmer, she has done much to promote the sport of swimming with her winning smile.

Pablo Morales provided inspiration to Olympic history. In 1984 he earned a silver medal in the 100 fly. In 1988 he did not qualify at the time trials for the Olympics. The swimming world assumed he was through competing. Three years later, at age 27, he took time off from law school to return to Stanford under the guidance of coach Skip Kenney. He set his sights on the 1992 Olympics in Barcelona. This time he won the gold! Today, Pablo is a role model for swimmers with public appearances demonstrating the use of the "monofin".

Swimming demands a commitment to excellence. The 1996 Olympics in Atlanta saw Amy Van Dyken collapse on deck with leg cramps after finishing fourth in a lifetime best time in the 100 meter freestyle. She came back to win gold medals in the 50 freestyle, 100 fly and relays. Tom Dolan emerged as the winner in the men's 400 IM but scratched a later event due to respiratory difficulties. Jeff Rouse, a veteran of

past Olympics, has been a dominant swimmer at the world level. But the elusive gold medal in the 100 backstroke at previous Olympics slipped past him until Atlanta. This time he won the event by almost a full second. Gary Hall, Jr. swam his fastest 50 freestyle to emerge one-tenth of a second behind Russia's Alexander Popov.

There were several firsts at the 1996 Olympics. Sheila Taormina at age 26 became the first Master swimmer to win a gold medal. Angel Martino was the oldest swimmer, at age 29, to win an Olympic gold medal. Jeff Rouse, age 26, was the oldest men's swimmer. Mary Ellen Clarke, age 32, overcame a battle with vertigo to win a bronze medal in platform diving. Swimmers are getting older.

What is in the future for swimming? Veterans such as Janet Evans will retire. Olympic newcomers Brooke Bennett and Amanda Beard will probably be back along with new faces. Four years is time enough for exercise physiologists to determine ways to make the body smoother, more slippery and faster.

Cyberspace is now the place to look for places to swim, workouts, latest meet results, swim books, videos and swim wear. See Chapter 5 for Internet locations. All you need is a computer with enough memory, a modem, and a Web browser.

A Day at the Races

Patsy Weiss, Rinconada Masters

Enjoying the spa after a meet

Middle: Florence Carr, St. Pete Masters

Swim Programs in the United States

3

The national governing body for amateur competitive swimming in the United States is USS or United States Swimming, Inc. It is a member of FINA (Federation Internationale de Natation Amateur - referring to the organization of amateur aquatics). FINA was founded in 1908 as the world-wide governing board to organize rules and regulations for swim competition, diving and water polo events. Synchronized swimming and later, Masters swimming were added to this umbrella.

FINA maintains world records for the above aquatic programs and is the governing body for organized aquatic events at the Olympics. FINA is responsible for drug testing of athletes involved in swim events.

The following aquatic sports have teams and clubs across the United States. Each sport requires different skills and offers the opportunity for competition.

Diving

This sport requires more knowledge of gymnastic moves than it does swimming skills. In fact, some of the top Olympic divers were gymnasts first. These individuals switched to diving following gymnastic injuries.

Two height options are allowed for competition events: 3-meter springboard and a 10-meter platform. Each requires different skills. In the springboard events, height in the air is achieved by flexibility of the board as well as execution skill. Dive height from the 10-meter platform is achieved by execution of the dive only.

The gymnastic moves used in dives are somersaults, twists, pikes and layouts. The dives themselves are placed in groups and performed in different positions. The diving groups are forward, backward, inward, reverse and twist performed in a free position. The positions are straight, pike or tuck. The 10-meter platform has a separate handstand category.

Competitors are required to do basic compulsory dives and optional dives of varying difficulty. Each optional dive is assigned a degree of difficulty dependent on the combination of moves. Entry into the water may be head first or feet first.

Divers are judged on take-off, execution of dive in the air, difficulty of dive and water entry. Judges use flash cards for score results. Scoring is from 1/2 point for a failed dive to a maximum of 10 points for a perfect dive.

United States Diving is organized into four different programs as it is taught in a progression of steps from the simplest to the most complex.

Junior division is for young children to learn the basics. Senior division is open to talented divers to further develop skills and compete at different levels. The International division is for exceptional divers to gain further experience. Master division is for divers over 21 who wish to continue diving for fun or competition.

Stephanie Straub

Sammy Lee, Pat McCormick, Jenny Chandler and Greg Louganis are a few outstanding American divers who popularized the sport. Greg is the most recent gold medal winner in both the 1984 and 1988 Olympics.

Diving encourages personal characteristics such as self-discipline, poise and commitment to improve. It provides an environment for working alone while being part of a larger team. At the 1996 Olympics in Atlanta Mary Ellen Clark earned a bronze medal in platform diving. To accomplish this feat, she had to overcome recurring bouts of vertigo which disturbed her sense of balance. Not an easy task for a diver!

Synchronized Swimming

Water ballet performed to music best describes this sport. To the observer, the moves look easy. In reality, it is the most difficult athletic exercise to master. Above average breath control, muscle strength and coordination are a few of the required skills. This sport combines gymnastic moves, dance artistry, and swimming skills.

A good knowledge of all strokes is necessary. Adaptations to these strokes may be used to fit the tempo of the music. Sculling is a basic arm movement used in most of the moves. The US Synchronized Swimming, Inc. recognizes eight different layout sculling positions. The rotary or "eggbeater" kick is used to gain height in the water for the ballet moves.

Synchronized swimming is a relatively new aquatic sport. Katherine Curtis founded the idea in 1923. In 1933 at the Chicago World's Fair, the first water show called synchronized swimming was presented. Water shows increased in popularity when Esther Williams swam to music in the movies during the late 1940's and 50's. It did not become one of the Olympic competitive events until 1992 at Barcelona.

There is the opportunity to perform solo, in pairs or as a team with 4 to 8 participants. Music is piped underwater so swimmers can move with the tempo of the music. Performances are judged on grace, interpretation of music, degree of difficulty and unison of swimmers. Artistic expression and choreography are important components of the aquatic routine.

Past Olympic gold medal winners in this sport were from California-trained teams. The Santa Clara Aquamaids and the Walnut Creek Aquanauts dazzled spectators with winners in solo and duet performances. According to Chris Carver, coach of the Santa Clara Aquamaids, team competition was allowed for the first time in the 1996 Olympics. The Aquamaids won a gold medal for their outstanding performance.

Today, the arena is changing with the addition of males in a female-dominated sport. Bill May, on the cover of this book, was a swimmer and gymnast prior to joining the Santa Clara Aquamaids. He performs a duet with Kristina Lum, also on the cover, that emphasizes how male strength can enhance ballet moves. Interestingly, Masters synchronized swimming has more male participants than females.

Water Polo

England is where water polo originated. In

1880, it became a team sport in the U States. Water polo uses a combination elements of soccer and rugby with goals, goalkeeper and seven players on each team. Rules are maintained by a referee who looks for underwater fouls. Originally, underwater play was permitted. The rules today require over-the-water play to reduce injuries and make it a spectator sport.

Swimmers use a modified freestyle arm action with the head above water. The kick is the rotary or "eggbeater" for height which is needed to pass the ball from one player to the next. Except for the goalie, swimmers cannot touch the bottom or sides of the pool during play.

Speed swimming and ball handling skills make for a fast-paced game. The number of girls playing water polo has increased rapidly in the last ten years at both the high school and college level. To give you an idea of the interest in girl's water polo, compare the following statistics. At the high school level in the Central Valley area of CA there were 4 teams in 1995, 19 teams in 1996 and 22 teams in 1997. Girls enjoy this sport because it is a new option for them to use swimming skills. According to Steve Baxter, Head Girl's Water Polo Coach at Clovis West High School in Clovis, CA, girls must learn to become physical to play this contact sport. The girls not only have to become aggressive but they have to learn how to focus on winning. After starting a team in 1996, his girls went on to win the 1997 Valley League Championships and were the CIF champions in the same year.

Stroke Competition

Competitive swimming involves dedication, endurance, relaxation, and a love of the water. Many hours will be spent in a chlorinated pool. On a hot summer day, it is a pleasure to get into the water. But, remember swimming is year around. The water is not as appealing on dark, wintry days. A good competitive program not only encourages winning but teaches youngsters how to lose gracefully.

There are opportunities to compete at many different levels. You may choose to swim with an age-group team. In this case you have the option of joining a summer swim league or a year around program.

Swimming with a team teaches cooperation, discipline, builds character and team bonding. Children compete within specific age-groups. The Junior division begins with the 8 and under age group, followed by 9–10, 11–12, 13–14, 15–16 and 1–18 age groups.

Laura Tonnesen

For the year around program, there are two racing seasons. Short course is the longest. It begins in September and ends in May. Race events during this season are swum in 25 yard distances. The events are as short as a 50 yard event and as long as a 200 yard event. Long course events extend from June through August and are swum in 50 meter distances. One lap of the pool would be a 50 meter event while a 200 meter swim would be 4 laps.

Pools in the United States are three different lengths to comply with official requirements. The lengths are 25 yards, 33 1/3 yards or 50 meters. The width of pools does not matter and will vary with space available. Newer pools utilize a movable bulkhead to adjust pool length for each season.

Sprint and distance workouts are offered during short and long course seasons. Sprint events require bursts of energy and power and require a special type of training. The distance events are directed toward the ability to pace for endurance. Both types of workouts enhance the body in different ways.

Four primary strokes are swum during competitive events—freestyle, backstroke, breaststroke, and butterfly. An event called the individual medley or IM is a combination of those four strokes swum in a prescribed order—butterfly, backstroke, breaststroke and freestyle.

Relays are part of competition. Four members make up a relay team. There are freestyle and medley relays for women, men and mixed teams. The format is the same as track relays. Each member swims one quarter of the total distance of the event and then is relieved by the next member. Team spirit and cooperation are generated during relays.

The training season whether in short or long course follows three phases. Each phase has a specific purpose and the workouts are geared toward that purpose.

Early season phase focuses on general body conditioning and lasts 6 to 8 weeks. All four strokes are prescribed in long, easy swims that build endurance. Stroke drills, breathing patterns and flip turns are built into the workout. Dry land exercises such as stretch cords or weight training augment the workout.

Mid-season phase is more specific to the goals of individual swimmers. Stroke and distance preference will vary among the team members. The workouts increase in distance and are high quality. This phase lasts 8 to 12 weeks.

Taper phase is performed prior to a competitive meet. It is the shortest phase, somewhere between 1 to 3 weeks. Quality workouts remain but total yardage for each workout is less. More rest is given between sets. Increased attention is spent on starts and turns. Think of this phase as fine tuning the body for a fast swim at the meet.

The opportunity to swim longer distances is available to young and old alike. Generally these swims are in a lake, ocean or river. Open water swims range from 1 to 5 miles, and include all age groups. Freestyle is the preferred stroke but it is not uncommon to see breaststroke swum for part of the distance. Either stroke allows the swimmer to look forward occasionally to check for landmarks.

Safety is a primary factor in open water swims. The starts are crowded as there may be 100 to 400 swimmers. Swimmers start off in waves with color-coded caps by age or swim time. Caps are required for visual identity. It behooves one to be alert to near by swimmers. It is no fun to accidently get hit or kicked by a passing swimmer.

Swimmers need to be concerned about currents, waves and water temperature. Hypothermia may set in any time the water temperature is below 70 degrees F (21 degrees C). It is life-threatening and affects conditioned and unconditioned swimmers.

Before attempting a long distance swim, practice in cold water. You may want to protect ears and head with multiple caps or a special insulated cap. Some races allow insulated wet suits. If not, apply vaseline to underarms, inner thighs and top of feet for insulation. It is common to feel dizzy when the body returns to an upright position at the finish. Walk slowly and wait for equilibrium to re-establish.

Within the last five years, the number of such events for younger children has increased dramatically. The longer the event, the more determination and focus is required. The body gets tired and swimming becomes mind over matter or sometimes mind over discomfort.

Instead of an age-group team, you may choose team swimming at the high school, junior college or four-year college level. High schools have their own separate leagues with regulations set by the High School Athletic Association. Each high school competes with several other local schools to make up a league. Championship meets are held at the end of the swim season.

At the college level there are two organizations that sponsor swimming and diving events. Two-year colleges are under The National Junior College Athletic Association founded in 1937 to promote sport activities. The National Collegiate Athletic Association (NCAA) was established to oversee sports at universities and four-year colleges in 1904. Both diving and swimming championships are sponsored by these organizations for men and women.

Basic Water Safety

Teaching swimming to children and adults is a great way to enjoy the water. Special swimming skills and certification are required for those individuals who wish to be lifeguards or teach swimming with an organization. Both the American Red Cross and the YMCA offer course work to learn the necessary skills. Addresses in your city can be obtained from the telephone book. You need to meet minimum age requirements for the different courses.

There are advantages to this training. One, you will learn teaching techniques to use at all age levels which may come in handy if you become a parent or enter teaching field. Second, you will always have a summer job. Third, it is to your advantage to be certificated to lessen any action by possible lawsuits.

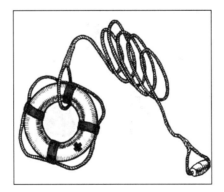

The A, B, Cs of Swimming

4

Acceleration through the water with minimum effort is the teaching aim of a good swim instructor or coach. Any object moving through water meets resistance from the water, called "drag". There are different types of drag. The position of arms and legs with respect to the torso may create drag; wave action creates turbulence drag and swim suits create frictional drag. To reduce drag, think of these four factors as you swim.

One, the body must be balanced which involves the position of the head to keep the body horizontal in the water. If the head is too high, the hips and/or legs drop and create drag. Another way to obtain balance is to think of pushing the chest forward and to the bottom of the pool. In swimming jargon, this action is called pressing the T. The cross of the T represents the chest from shoulder to shoulder. The vertical line represents the sternum. Press down where the two intersect. You should feel as if you are swimming downhill, but in effect, the hips are riding high which is good.

Two, the body must be streamlined as possible to keep body form narrow. The best divers and swimmers are always stretched out into a streamlined position. A body that is long and straight creates less turbulence in the air and water. To achieve this position, keep the lower body in alignment with the shoulders. Don't wiggle the hips or head from side to side.

When swimming freestyle or backstroke, the hips rotate from left to right and drive the shoulders with them. This motion is entirely different from a wiggle. Think of moving your hips out of the way as each hand passes through the water.

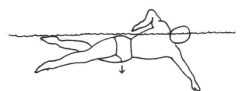

Hip rotation

Always streamline while executing the stroke, while pushing off the wall after a turn, and while diving off the blocks. A good streamline start and turn off the wall can take seconds off your time.

Streamlining makes you feel long and smooth. The object of a good swimmer is to take as few strokes as possible by getting maximum distance from each arm stretch and pull back. Beginning swimmers will sacrifice smoothness for speed. They not only look choppy but will tire sooner.

Try this drill for learning to increase distance with each stroke. First, swim an easy timed 50 yard freestyle and count the number of strokes on each lap. Second, repeat the process but try to swim faster and still hold the same stroke count. If you can't, try rotating the hips more and sooner or alter body position for better balance. You can increase kick speed to go faster, but you will tire sooner.

Alexander Popov and Gary Hall, Jr. are the fastest 50 meter freestylers in the world. Both swimmers have a low stroke count. Every time they take an arm stroke they move their bodies farther in the water than anyone else.

Three, cut through the water. Smooth, angled arm entry followed by long arm strokes reduces wave turbulence. The front part of the stroke is crucial for streamlining but the final part of the arm stroke provides the most propulsion, along with hip rotation.

With a high elbow enter the hand, angled with thumb entering first, followed by fingers. The palm should be facing outward from the body. This position is necessary for the "catch" phase. Continue to extend the arm under water while rotating the hip to the bottom of the pool. At this point you

Palm away from body

Catch

should be on your side, one hip and shoulder facing the bottom of the pool and the other hip and shoulder facing the top of the water. Grab water with outturned palm. Make an insweep motion of the hand. This means the hand is rotated so the palm faces the feet. Push this water toward the chest, then waist and past the hips. The arm must be bent 90 degrees at the elbow to keep the arm under the body while executing this part of the stroke. Once the hand passes the hip, the hand must rotate outward and upward for the recovery phase.

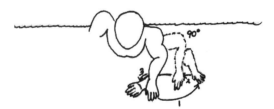

Arm Pull Motions

Swimming is a "feel" sport. To feel the importance of the hand as it catches and pulls water past the hips try this drill. Swim one lap with closed fists, then open the hands to normal position for the next lap. Sense the difference in the ability to pull water.

When swimming any stroke keep the elbows high with a bent forearm. This allows the shoulders to ride high above the water to further reduce drag. Any part of the body out of the water means less resistance in the water.

High elbows

Four, reduce frictional drag by making the body smooth. Wear a suit that hugs the body. One bathing suit style designed to smooth out body contours is used by all ages, male and female. This is the body suit with a high neck, zipper down the back and high leg cut. Older swimmers use this suit to contain loose, wrinkled skin for a smoother feel in the water. Other suit styles are designed with an open back and high cut leg for females and a bikini suit style for men. Wear a bathing cap to make the head smooth.

Frictional drag may be created by a hairy body. For this reason, competitive swimmers may choose to shave the head and or the body to obtain a sleek feel as they move through the water.

Breathing and *buoyancy* are skills that make swimming easier. To learn these skills you need to be relaxed. A relaxed body is supported by the water and will float. Fear of the water prevents beginning swimmers from attaining a relaxed attitude. I think of the water as a mattress holding me up while I stretch out on my stomach. In this position, take a breath by barely turning the head to get the mouth above water. Breathing out underwater is necessary and should be a relaxed response. Tense swimmers tend to hold their breath underwater which means air must be expelled and taken in when the head is turned the next time. Very soon the swimmer can't fill the lungs with sufficient air and he or she becomes more tense. Learning to relax in the water takes time and the patience of a good instructor. Confidence between pupil, water, and the instructor must develop before this skill is mastered.

Three **Cs** are needed by the swimmer to master swim strokes or perfect dives: *concentration, commitment* and *coordination.* The four basic strokes—freestyle, backstroke, breaststroke and butterfly—have some elements in common and some differences. Concentration on where one part of the body is in relation to other parts is important. You must feel the water against body parts.

Arm action in all four strokes is divided into four distinct phases: *entry, catch, pull,* and *recovery.* This pattern is used for alternating arms in free and backstroke and double arms in breaststroke and butterfly.

In the *entry* the fingertips are first, followed by the hand. At this point the hand should feel the pressure of water. The second phase is to continue arm entry while the hand sculls outward to *catch* water. Third phase is to *pull* this water with the hand and forearm under the stomach and past the thigh. To have a streamlined, powerful pull, the forearm is bent 90 degrees at the elbow. This part of the stroke should propel the body forward. The *recovery* phase is to bring a relaxed arm out of the water, elbow first and return in the air for the next entry.

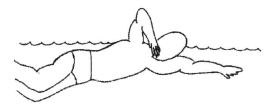

The kick in freestyle is the flutter kick. The leg action comes from the hip not by bending at the knee. If executed properly, only the heel will break the surface of the water. Depth between the two kicks should be 10 to 12 inches. The kick is for balance, although a faster kick will propel the swimmer faster. The power in freestyle comes from the arm action.

The kick in the backstroke is similar to freestyle in that it is generated from the hips, and is for balance. The down part of the kick should be emphasized, and is accomplished by a slightly bent knee. A relaxed up beat will allow only the tips of the toes to break the water's surface.

The breaststroke kick is a movement of propulsion through the water, not for balance. It is as important as the arms for power. A good kick requires rotation of the knees so that the ankles remain outside the knees. Some individuals may have knee joints that prevent this type of motion. To begin the kick, bend the lower legs toward the buttocks with the soles of the feet always under water. With knees pointed toward the bottom of the pool, rotate knees so that lower legs move outward. Pressure of the water should be felt on the inside of the foot and leg. The power of the kick is to thrust the feet back together while straightening the legs.

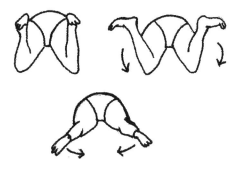

The coordination of this stroke is in two parts: start the arm pull first and coordinate the kick so that it propels the body forward as the arms recover.

In butterfly the dolphin kick is for propulsion. It is an undulating kick executed by a lift of the hips and a snap of the ankles. The difficult part is to coordinate the kick with the arms and breathing. Actually there are two kicks for every arm pull, one stronger than the other.

Breathing must be coordinated with the arm pull. The head is propelled up and forward as the arms begin to pull back. It takes time to learn all these skills. Remember, you can concentrate only on one or two parts of the stroke at any given session. For most people, it is best not to attempt to learn the whole stroke at once. Perfect each part, then move ahead to the next phase.

At the end of a long day, July 1996

John Selmer, age 50, successfully completes swimming the English Channel.

Beginner Swim Progression

1. HOLD BREATH 10 SECONDS
2. RHYTHMIC BREATHING
3. PRONE FLOAT — push off
4. PRONE GLIDE
5. SURVIVAL FLOATING 1 MINUTE
6. BACK GLIDE — push off
7. PRONE GLIDE WITH KICK
8. BACK GLIDE WITH KICK
9. CRAWL STROKE OR BEGINNER STROKE 20 YARDS
10. COMBINED STROKE ON BACK 15 YARDS
11. CHANGE DIRECTION
12. TURNING OVER
13. JUMPING IN
14. SAFETY SKILLS
15. COMBINED SKILLS CHECKS

Adapted from the American Red Cross

When, Where and How to Start Swimming

5

The earlier swim instruction starts the better for several reasons. One, it is a safety factor for young children, particularly in areas where there are pools or lakes. In California alone, approximately 900 drownings of children between the ages of one and five occur each year. These deaths can be prevented by parent and child both learning basic safety skills. Also, children are less self-conscious about learning to swim prior to the age of seven or eight.

Preschool instruction is offered through swim schools, private instruction and organizations such as the YMCA and American Red Cross. Parent/child classes are meaningful for children under three years of age. Certain qualities are essential when choosing an instructor for this age group. The teacher needs to like children, be patient but firm, and utilize child psychology when necessary. Look for an experienced teacher. Getting off to a good start in the water is as important as getting off to a good start in kindergarten. Both situations will have an effect on the desire to continue to learn.

Putting the face in the water and sinking to the bottom of the pool are universal reasons why children and adults don't learn to swim. These fears are real and can make swim lessons traumatic! Private sessions are better for these individuals. Call swim schools, check want ads in the newspaper and ask other people for instructor referrals.

The second reason for learning to swim early centers around body development. Certain pathways are established in the brain when skills are learned early on. These pathways can be re-established later, even after a twenty-year hiatus. The brain is more flexible from preschool through high school than it is later in life. This is why children and young adults learn skills quickly compared to older adults. Also, bad habits and poor swimming technique are more difficult to correct as one ages. Why not learn the correct technique from the start?

It is common for young children to forget how to swim from one year to the next, especially if the opportunity to practice stops over the winter months. Usually one or two refresher lessons will quickly get the child back in swimming form.

As children reach elementary school age there are many places to learn to swim. The YMCA has a strong swimming program across the United States for all ages. They provide training programs for their instructors. A child can learn to swim here and move up the ladder to eventually become an instructor. The American Red Cross also trains instructors to teach at recreation centers and swim camps.

Swim camps are a great place to have fun. You can learn safety skills, boating, and improve swim technique all at the same time. Camps are offered through many youth organizations, recreation centers and even at universities during the summer.

Summer League programs are another way to learn and have fun at the same time. Most communities offer programs through their recreation departments, country clubs or home pool associations.

There are separate magazines for different types of swimming that offer nutritional advice, places to swim, equipment and sample workouts. *Swim Magazine*, published bimonthly by Sports Publication, Inc., 228 Nevada St., El Segundo, CA 90245, is directed toward the adult swimmer with a special insert specifically for Master Swimming. Other sport magazines can be obtained by writing to the addresses at the end of this chapter.

Use the Internet for swimming list links. All connections begin with http://, followed by specific numbers and letters. This is the protocol format for an Internet address. To reach the following sites, type in the address and press enter. (All addresses below begin with http://).

Swimmer's Guide Online:
205.159.83.130:80/~SGOL

A database with over 3,000 places to swim in the United States.

Harvard Swimming Links:
hcs.harvard.edu/~meNswim/links/

Several links to specific sites to swim as well as workout schedules and contact people.

Peak Performance Swim Clinics Camps:
www.worldwideswim.com

List clinics and camps. Weekly customized workouts. CD-ROM with workouts, log book, stroke tips by Olympians.

Swimming World/Swim Technique Magazine:
www.swim.info.com

Online catalog of swimming books and videos.

NorCal Swim Shop:
www.swim shop.com/

Swim wear and equipment catalog.

Terry Laughlin's Total Immersion:
www.totalimmersion.pair.com

Articles on efficient swimming. Videos, books and equipment for sale.

Swimming Science Journal:

rohan.sdsu.edu/dept/coachsci/swimming/index.html

Analytical information on strokes, good for coaches.

US Swimming:

www.usswim.org

Training diaries of several Olympic swimmers. History of swimming.

The following sites apply to Master programs.

FINA Index:

www.fina.org/

FINA rules, records, newsletter, World Championship information.

The World of Masters Swimming:

www.hk.super.net/~kff/wms.html

World Master records and humorous anecdotes.

United States Master Swimming:

www.usms.org

Mountain View Masters:

www.mvm.org/

Workouts are updated weekly. Good for technique and conditioning.

Pacific Masters Swimming:

www.pacificmasters.org

Results from national Master meets. Swim sites, vendors, equipment.

Communities advertise swim programs through their recreation departments. If this route is not successful, addresses for different water activities are listed below.

US Diving, Inc.
Pan American Plaza
201 S. Capitol Ave., Ste. 430
Indianapolis, IN 46225

US Water Polo
Pan American Plaza
201 S. Capital Ave., Ste. 520
Indianapolis, IN 46225

US Synchronized Swimming
Pan American Plaza
210 S. Capitol Ave., Ste. 510
Indianapolis, IN 46225

US Masters Swimming
2 Peter Avenue
Rutland, MA 01543

USS Swimming
Olympic Training Center
1750 E. Boulder St.
Colorado Springs, CO 80909

YMCA Swim Programs
Oakbrook Square
6083–AA Oakbrook Pkwy.
Norcross/Atlanta GA 30093

American Red Cross
17th and D Streets N.W.
Washington, D.C. 20006

Above: Michelle Tonneson. Below: Jason and Michael Callison with the author.

Nutrition as it Relates to Physical Fitness

6

Swimmers like to eat! One of the reasons swimmers join a club is that the exercise allows them "to eat whatever they want". The prospect of enjoying a good breakfast or lunch is a bonus that goes along with workouts.

The slogan "what we eat is what we are" must be kept in mind if performance and efficiency are goals. Swimmers need to find combinations of foods that will provide substantial carbohydrates for energy, protein for muscle and tissue repair, plus fat for cell metabolism and alternate energy needs.

Nutritionists like to design food pyramids as a way of presenting a quick visual approach to the ratio of food groups eaten by people.

Below are three pyramids. The USDA pyramid contains new guidelines formulated in 1992. Fruits and vegetables are given a higher percentage than the old guidelines. The Asian and Mediterranean pyramids are the result of a collaboration between a Boston think tank, Oldways Preservation & Exchange Trust, and the Harvard School of Public Health.

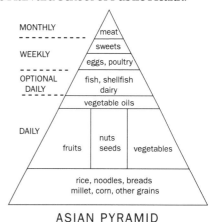

ASIAN PYRAMID

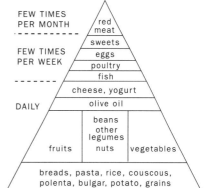

MEDITERRANEAN PYRAMID

USDA PYRAMID

The purpose of pyramids is to get people to think in terms of percentages of food groups rather than ounces. The president of the think tank suggests combining all three approaches. K. Dun Gifford says, "Eat like a Mediterranean three days a week. Eat like an Asian three days a week. And on the seventh day have a steak and Haagen-Dazs."

Another way to look at these percentages is the original, broad dietary goal recommended by the American Dietetic Association (USDA) for daily nutrients.

- 58–60% of kcalories in carbohydrate
- 12–15% of kcalories in protein
- 20–30% of kcalories in fat

A *kcalorie* is the commonly used measurement for potential energy in nutrients.

Different percentages for the above food groups are recommended by different sources. Barry Sears, author of the book, *The Zone*, recommends 30% fat, 30% protein and 40% carbohydrates. His recommenda-

tion is from research on heart disease and energy requirements. The Stanford swim team has used this approach successfully for a few years.

Which set of percentages is the best? You have to answer that question. The purchase of a good nutrition book along with a record of what you eat and how you feel will help determine the best percentage for high energy level and weight maintenance.

One of the best approaches to a diet that furnishes a high energy level is explained by Sally Edwards in her book *Heart Rate Monitor*. Sally is a triathlete who gives motivational talks on the value of exercise. She uses running as an example but a swim workout could replace the run.

Let's say you eat high carbohydrate meals for one day. Note the number of hours slept. The next morning do a workout of your choice that is timed. Write down the time of day, distance, stroke, times and total yardage. Include how you felt—peppy, tired, slow. Rest for a day. Then change your diet by adjusting to high protein or fat meals for one day. Sleep the same hours as before. Do the exact same workout at the same time of day as before and compare times and how you feel. Continue this procedure until you determine a ratio of food intake that allows you to achieve peak performances and feel good at the same time.

It is important to keep a record of results and not rely on memory. Try extending this procedure to a week at a time. The point to be taken is everyone has a different cell metabolism. It makes sense to find the ratio of food groups that best suits your needs.

The ratio of muscle to fat in the athlete is important for peak performance. Muscle tissue demands more energy than fat tissue. It has a higher rate of metabolism than fat, therefore it burns more calories. The more muscle one has, the greater potential for mechanical work. Fat does not provide mechanical work but it does supply fuel for energy needs.

Protein is composed of necessary amino acids needed by cells to make muscle tissue. There is no way to force extra protein into muscles to make them grow larger just by eating additional protein. Protein intake into cells is regulated by hormones plus the demand of exercise placed on them. As one exercises, cells pull amino acids in from the blood, provided there is adequate protein in the diet.

Muscle contractions require a source of energy in the form of ATP molecules. Much of the energy (ATP molecules) needed for sprinting is provided by a fuel source called creatine phosphate. Protein is needed to produce creatine. In muscles, creatine is synthesized into creatine phosphate where it acts as a special energy carrier for the continuous production of ATP. As creatine phosphate supplies are depleted, glucose, glycogen and fats provide the fuel for ATP production.

The quantity of protein one needs depends on the amount of lean muscle tissue in the body and the amount of daily exercise performed. Fat tissue requires very little protein to maintain itself, but muscles and blood must be maintained by a continuous supply of essential amino acids. To determine a rough estimate of your protein needed *per day*, calculate the following.

1. Multiply your weight by 1kg /2.2lbs. For example: my weight is 116 lbs.

$$16 \times \frac{1kg}{2.2} = 52.7 \text{ grams protein needed}$$

Americans are more accustomed to buying food in ounces rather than grams. To make the above figure realistic, note that 1 ounce equals about 28 grams. Because swimmers may have more lean muscle tissue, protein needed per day may be higher than the rough estimate.

Body fat can be determined several ways. One accurate but inconvenient way is the submersion test in water which must be performed in a laboratory setting. A second way is by a bioelectrical impedance test which attaches electrodes to the hand and foot to send a harmless radio frequency wave through the body. This wave measures water content and that number provides a guide to body fat. This apparatus has appeared at swim meets and is correct within a 2 to 3 percent margin of error. Exercise and liquid intake may alter the results. A third, simple but fairly accurate way is to calculate body mass index, using body weight and height. Heavily muscular individuals may have a high reading, indicating false obesity. This test, called a BMI, is an index of body fat that corrects for height.

A healthy BMI is 19 - 25. To determine your BMI, calculate the following:

1. Multiply your weight in pounds by 0.45
2. Multiply your height in inches by 0.025
3. Square the answer from Step 2
4. Divide the answer from Step 1 by the answer from Step 3

For example:

1. my weight of 116 x 0.45 = 52.2
2. my height of 64 x 0.025 = 1.60
3. square 1.60 (1.60 x 1.60) = 2.56
4. 52.2 / 2.56 = 20.3 is my BMI

A high BMI, above 25, would indicate calories exceed energy needs. The body does not get rid of nutrients; they are stored in the form of fat in special fat cells located strategically throughout the body.

Fat is used for fuel by muscles but can be broken down only as long as oxygen is available. Therefore, fat deposits supply energy for moderate activity but not for strenuous activity such as sprints. But there is a bright side to strenuous physical conditioning that a good swim program provides. Strenuous swimming conditions muscles to burn more fat as fuel by encouraging the build up of fat-metabolizing machinery in the cell. Conditioned muscles will burn fat longer at a higher activity level than poorly conditioned muscles. This is one reason athletes maintain weight levels.

Carbohydrates are the primary source of energy for all body cells. These are the starches and sugars found in fruit, pasta, bread or grains. The fuel of muscle cells is not protein but carbohydrate and fat which is converted into glucose for cell use. During strenuous activity, cells use this glucose and a storage-form called glycogen. During rest periods, glucose is stored as glycogen for future needs.

Nutritionists agree that people who exercise strenuously should consume carbohydrates within thirty minutes after physical activity to refuel "spent" muscles. Glucose is converted rapidly into glycogen because enzymes within muscle cells are most active during this time period. Even if you are not hungry, drink fruit juice. Eat a granola or sport's bar to replace depleted glycogen supplies. An apple, banana, dried fruit or bagel is a good source of nourishment. At this time, you should consume half a gram of carbohydrate per pound of body weight.

Swimmers should consume a high percentage of carbohydrates daily to store maximum amounts of glycogen to ward off fatigue during strenuous workouts. It should be noted that it takes the body about 48 hours to restore muscle carbohydrate to its pre-exercise level following a highly strenuous workout or endurance event. Continue to consume carbohydrate snacks every two hours for up to eight hours after a hard workout. This means a 150 pound person would consume 300 calories at each snack. The recommendation to work out hard one day and rest the next day makes sense. Also, rest a day or so before a swim meet and eat a carbohydrate-rich diet.

There are many athletic diets advertised to improve energy level. Whether they work for you depends on many factors including the side effects of changing cell metabolism (muscle pain, cardiac pain, weight gain). Carbohydrate loading, a technique designed to induce muscles to store more glycogen by manipulating carbohydrate levels, has it share of side effects on heart action. The best advice is eat a diet consistently high in carbohydrate, especially before competitive meets to keep muscle glycogen levels elevated. Maintaining a consistent weight is an indicator that energy expenditure and caloric intake are in balance.

Liquids

Liquid intake is as important to muscle metabolism as are carbohydrates. Muscles heat up during activity. An adequate fluid intake is important to maintain a high plasma volume so blood can penetrate muscles and carry the heat away. During heavy exertion and following exertion, blood supplies oxygen and nutrients to muscles for energy metabolism. High fluid intake ensures adequate electrolytes to prevent muscle cramps and to permit sweating.

When plasma volume decreases, water is pulled from all body cells to compensate for the loss, resulting in dehydration. Athletes become fatigued as dehydration occurs. A headache following a workout or competition may be the result of dehydration in brain and muscle cells.

Thirst is not a reliable sign for swimmers that more water is needed. Humans are the only mammals that do not have reliable dehydration signals. Actually, if you are thirsty, it is too late - your body is giving signals of impending dehydration. Being in a water environment gives a false sense that the body is cool. In reality, swimmers still sweat, and lose considerable water through increased respiration rates and metabolic processes. Swimmers may lose up to a quart of water or more per hour on a warm day.

To counteract dehydration, drink fluids before, during, and after workout. Drink as much fluid in cold weather as warm weather. On a cold day you have to warm and moisten the air as you inhale. Bring a water bottle to your workout lane and sip between sets. The same is true at meets. Drink as much fluid as you can before the meet and replenish fluid intake between events. This action will help to prevent sore muscles and a headache the following day. If you are really concerned about fluid volume, avoid caffeine and alcohol as they both encourage kidneys to eliminate water from plasma.

Carbohydrate-high sports drinks can be used to replenish muscle fuel and ward off dehydration. Read labels carefully. Some contain high sugar levels that irritate the stomach. Others lack vitamins and minerals needed by body cells. Water is still the preferred choice of liquid.

Supplements

Should I take vitamins and minerals to enhance my diet?, This is a question asked by many people. A well-balanced diet probably supplies all necessary vitamins for the average physically active person. Well-balanced means following daily recommended amounts in the food pyramid.

Research indicates that increased oxygen consumed during strenuous exertion results in the build up of highly reactive molecules in body cells called free radicals. These molecules are the result of normal metabolic reactions involving oxygen. Because these molecules result in an unpaired electron at their surface, they damage cells or damage the machinery in cells as they attach and enter the cell. Antioxidant vitamins such as A, C, and E have the ability to interfere with the reactivity of the free radical, and thus reduce damage to cells. There has been substantial research to prove the effectiveness of these vitamins to limit free radical damage. For additional information on free radicals, read Chapter 13.

Vitamin E is a constituent of the cell membrane and prevents the free radical from gaining entrance to the cell. Sources of foods that contain Vitamin E are peanut butter, almonds, sunflower seeds, fish and vegetable oils. Taking vitamin E in the natural form or in supplements strengthens the immune system.

Vitamin C acts as a sentry in the body, surrounding and protecting valuable substances such as iron from oxidation. Iron is needed for healthy red blood cells. Vitamin C can grab and hold onto this substance, ensuring its absorption from the intestinal tract into blood vessels. In the process, Vitamin C is oxidized but iron is saved. Just take more Vitamin C the next day.

Sources of Vitamin C in foods include fruits such as strawberries, tomatoes, kiwis, honeydew and cantaloupe melons, citrus fruits. Vegetables that contain Vitamin C are brussel sprouts, cabbage, kale, red and green peppers and potatoes.

Vitamin A and C are important to the formation of the protein collagen which is needed to build healthy body tissues. The immune system, which is made up of various cells and tissue, is boosted by Vitamin C for this reason. During heavy exercise, cells are injured and need to be replaced. The immune system carries away the dead cells to make way for new replacements. Linus Pauling, Nobel prize researcher, recommended megadoses of this vitamin to ward off the common cold and cancer. As one ages, the immune system may need a "push" to stay efficient. Vitamin C is thought to provide the push.

Coenzyme Q-10 is a popular supplement recommended by health firms to enhance body metabolism and destroy free radicals. The body manufactures this substance naturally. Its function is to aid cell enzymes and to act as an antioxidant in the cell. It is found in nuts, fish, and vegetable oils. According to the October, 1996 UC Berkeley Wellness Letter, substantial research has not been performed on this coenzyme to warrant its addition to the diet. At this time no one knows what elevated levels will accomplish in the body.

Swimmers want to remain healthy by avoiding microbes and viruses that cause colds and flu. Echinacea purpurea is an herb capable of strengthening the immune system, thereby lessening symptoms of the common cold. It is available in tablet, liquid or as tea from health food stores. Limited research in Germany indicates it boosts the number of white blood cells in circulation to increase the effectiveness of the immune system for approximately 10 days. It should be taken only when a cold is coming on and for 10 days thereafter.

Information from the November 1993 U C *Berkeley Wellness Letter,* states nine species of this herb are grown in the United States. It is more commonly known as the purple cone-flower, part of the sunflower family. No harmful side effects have been reported with its use.

Swimmers' Favorite Activity

Getting Stoked: Energy Foods

Physical Conditioning

7

Many changes occur to the body in the process of becoming physically fit. Most of the changes center around an increase in the efficiency of oxygen transporting mechanisms. This is why exercise is touted as a way to reduce heart disease. The changes occur over several months, dependent on age and amount of exercise performed. If one begins an exercise program later in life, the conditioning process may take longer but it will happen!

With regular, strenuous exercise that swim workouts promote, the respiratory system becomes more efficient at taking in air and expelling carbon dioxide. As more air is inhaled, oxygen molecules are extracted and incorporated into a growing number of red blood cells. Growth of small blood vessels into muscle and organs occurs to quickly transport oxygen molecules to these areas.

Metabolism within muscle cells changes as exercise continues. Mechanisms to attract and hold on to oxygen increase. The energy producing machinery within the cell, mito-chondria, increase in numbers. Mitochondria use glucose and oxygen to manufacture ATP molecules, a source of stored energy for mechanical, chemical and electrical work within the body.

The more conditioned a person is, the more energy molecules are produced for the increased exercise level. Conditioned muscle cells burn fat longer, saving glycogen stores for future glucose needs. In spite of what Covert Bailey, author of *Fit or Fat*, says, regular, strenuous swimming will encourage weight loss if caloric intake is also monitored.

Energy for Muscle Work

Body cells can only use glucose for energy sources. Glucose may be derived from carbohydrates or fats. Carbohydrates are the preferred choice because they do not produce acidic by-products. Excess carbohydrates are stored as glycogen (limited storage) or as fat. Protein can be broken down to supply glucose but this process will only happen if insufficient carbohydrates or fats are available.

Within the muscle cell, glucose is broken down in a multistep process to produce energy. Oxygen may or may not be available for this process, depending on the type of workout performed. Sprint workouts result in deficient amounts of oxygen to cells while distance workouts that are paced provide a constant supply of oxygen. As the swimmer becomes conditioned, changes within the cardiovascular system make muscle metabolism much more efficient and able to tolerate less oxygen.

There are three distinct types of energy systems going on within the cell. First is the *aerobic* type which means with oxygen. Then there is the *anaerobic* system which means without oxygen. This statement is misleading because the cell is never completely devoid of oxygen or it would die. During this system, there is a build-up of a chemical by-product called lactic acid which interferes with efficient muscle metabolism. Last, is the *anaerobic alactic type* which means there is still deficient oxygen supplies but the duration is very short, and the cell has learned to handle the build-up of lactic acid.

The *aerobic* process is the most efficient because it provides muscle cells with sufficient oxygen to completely break down glucose to water and carbon dioxide and it produces lots of energy molecules. This energy system is used in a paced workout - let's say 3 X 500 yard freestyle. Aerobic systems provide sufficient oxygen to muscle cells so that sustained exercise can be performed over long periods of time. Conditioned muscles do not tire readily when

there is sufficient oxygen delivered to cells.

If oxygen is not delivered fast enough to muscle cells, they break glucose down as far as they can and kick into the *anaerobic* phase. Lactic acid will now be produced as a waste product. The accumulation of lactic acid during periods of "oxygen debt" changes the acid balance in muscle cells which contributes to fatigue. This energy system is used in a sprint workout where the rest interval between sets of 50 yard freestyle is short. Anaerobic systems supply a lot of energy but operate for a short period of time.

The body's disposal of lactic acid is of interest to the performing athlete. Oxygen is needed to break down the accumulated lactic acid. Swimmers increase respiration rate to bring in the necessary oxygen. Swimming an easy 50 or 100 yards after a hard set accomplishes this purpose.

In the well conditioned athlete, fatigue is delayed when the *anaerobic alactic* energy system kicks in for a short time period as muscle cells get accustomed to a lactic acid increase. To use this system, swim all out for 12 1/2 yards, then slow down to the end of the pool. Repeat 10 times. As the circulatory system increases in efficiency, oxygen is delivered faster to muscle cells, and lactic acid is broken down more rapidly.

In training it is important to have workouts that utilize each of the energy systems. Good body conditioning will be the ultimate result. This is why a coach is vital to the overall success of a good exercise program. He or she should have the ability to design workouts which train muscles and the cardiovascular system to be as efficient as possible.

Weight Training and Flexibility Exercises

"Loss of strength is inevitable with aging". "Resistance training is dangerous for older people". One by one these previously accepted assumptions are being disproved. For the average American, muscle mass does start decreasing 2% each year after age 30. For sedentary individuals the loss is greater. Are swimmers typical average Americans? Not in the category of physical activity levels.

Research on older individuals indicates that muscle mass can be increased by a weight training program started at any age. Data also indicates that increased strength leads to improved balance and functional mobility.

Personally, I have observed a couple, now in their early 90's, who have been taking a weight training class for the last 15 years. Both the man and woman can "bench press" more weight than some college students in the class, and more than I can. The woman pushes 260 pounds on the Universal leg machine. Maria A. Fiatarone, MD performing research at the US Department of Agriculture Human Nutrition Research Center on Aging at Tufts University confirms that people over 85 benefit rapidly, within 2 to 3 weeks of starting a weight program.

Of the 60 Master swimmers interviewed, only 10% do not use any type of cross training to enhance physical fitness level. Approximately 30% of the swimmers use weights to gain swimming strength. Generally, this activity is performed 2 to 3 days a week on nonswimming days.

Experts differ in their opinions about what type of equipment to use. Some believe free weights are the best because the subject performs many of the exercises while standing. Balance increases and bone strength may be increased as the muscles work to stabilize the upright body. Free weights encourage multiple joint movements—wrist, elbow, shoulder or ankle, knee, and hip. Swimming mechanics incorporate the same multiple joint action. Free weights do not limit range of motion. They require guidance from a qualified instructor because awareness to body position is important to perform the motion correctly. Weights done incorrectly can lead to injuries!

Machine weights (Nautilus, Cybex) predetermine the range of motion. There is less chance of injury using this equipment compared to free weights. This type of training is probably best for beginners. Some machine weights are aimed at isolating one joint movement or one muscle. The choice of free weights or machine weights may depend on availability and cost.

Most age-group and college swimmers work out with weights as recommended by their respective coaches. Usually the weight training is part of their regular routine. For Master swimmers, weight training is an optional activity.

After college your lifestyle will determine

how often to work out. If you can manage a 30 to 45 minute workout 2 to 3 times a week, that is great.

Weights are performed in sets of repetitions. A "rep" is repeating a particular movement 8, 10 or 15 times at relatively high intensity. The recommended number of sets necessary for muscle strength used to be 2 or 3 with a 2 to 4 minute rest between sets. In the University of California Wellness Letter, January 1996, research at University of Florida and Penn State indicates that athletes who performed one set experienced similar improvements in muscle strength and size as the athletes that performed three sets.

Nancy Rideout, Masters swimmer, confirms that weight training improves swim times. She started a weight program for the first time in June of 1995, age 53, prior to the US Long Course Nationals in Gresham, Oregon. She trained 3 times a week for 1 and 1/2 hour sessions under the guidance of a trainer. Both free and machine weights were used. Her times at Nationals were the best she had swum in three years.

Betsy Jordan, Masters swimmer, can attest to the advantage of doing weights on upper body strength. She started free and mechanical weights 6 years ago. She works out 3 times a week for about 45 minutes. This regime translated into faster times, especially sprint times. See Chapter 11, section on swimmer training routines with specific weights.

In the Appendix there is a sample of free weight exercises designed by Norman Manoogian of Foothill Community College, Los Altos Hills, CA. These exercises specifically strengthen muscles and joints used by swimmers. The sets and reps are guidelines that can be adjusted for each person's time frame. Most individuals perform at least two sets of selected parts of the exercises one day and finish the remaining exercises on another day.

Stretch cords are another popular form of cross training. Swimmers feel most clubs have enough space to set up stretch cords for a 10 to 15 minute stretch session. Dry land activities help the older swimmer remain flexible. Even though water is gentler on the body than most sports, swimmers agree that as one ages it is important to stretch slowly and gently to prevent injuries. The older swimmers (70 to 80 age groups) such as Jean Durston, Jae Howell and Aldo Da Rosa perform extensive stretching routines throughout the day, starting before rising from bed. See the section on training routines of Master swimmers in Chapter 11.

Jim Miller, coach of Virginia Masters, offers a yearly clinic with the help of an exercise physiologist on the use of weight training and stretch cords.

Aaron Mattes of the Aaron Mattes Therapy Clinic in Sarasota, Florida has a new book out on *Active Isolated Stretching* that would be valuable to swimmers. The ideas are different from the previous technique of holding a stretch for 20 to 30 seconds. He maintains that athletes should hold the stretch at the point of light strain for 2 seconds, then relax for 2 seconds and repeat this cycle for 12 times. Muscles have a natural tendency to tighten up again after two seconds of stretching so holding for 20 seconds or longer aggravates the natural contractile reflex.

In older swimmers, the legs are the first part of the body to decline in efficiency. Rinconada Masters Swim Team in Palo Alto, CA, has a two foot deep, separate pool where part of the swim warm-up includes running in water prior to entering the workout pool. This activity serves as a partial warm-up while providing the non-runner with good leg exercise. The water offers substantial resistance to build up leg muscle and enhance flexibility.

Biking, running and walking are ways that swimmers improve leg strength and cardiovascular fitness. At age 80 Dexter Woodford, O*H*I*O* Masters, incorporates walking with swimming at least 5 days a week. To celebrate his 80th birthday he combined a swim, walk routine from 7:00 AM to 5:45 PM that totaled 21 miles. Way to go, Dexter! Anne McGuire, Gold Coast Masters, runs about 5 miles, 4 times a week for additional exercise. Running may not improve swimming times but it does improve overall physical fitness, particularly the cardiovascular system.

Dexter Woodford

Shoulder Injuries

Overuse or incorrect stroke technique are common reasons for shoulder injuries. The first sign of a problem is discomfort in and around the shoulder joint or pain in the upper arm muscles when the arm is raised over the head or raised laterally. The underlying cause for the discomfort may be inflammation of a tendon that attaches muscle to bone. Or one of several fluid filled sacs in the shoulder joint called bursae are inflamed. Recommended treatment is rest and ice pack application. If left untreated, rotator cuff injury may develop.

Rotator cuff injuries occur in swimmers due to strain placed on the shoulder joint. The problem may start as tendinitis, bursitis or a separate injury. The rotator cuff is four muscles with their tendons that control range of motion involving the upper arm bone or humerus. The supraspinatus, infraspinatus, teres minor and subscapularis, originate on the scapula bone, and their tendons encircle the head of the humerus. Generally, a tear occurs in the connective tissue of the tendons, referred to as a rotator cuff injury. The shoulder joint is no longer stabilized.

The following exercises, if performed regularly, may help prevent shoulder injury by strengthening the muscles and tendons. These exercises are taken from the UC Berkeley Wellness Letter, August 1994.

SHOULDER STRETCH
One arm on shoulder. Grasp arm, fingers toward body. Gently pull the arm away from body for 15 seconds. Repeat 5 times.

SHOULDER STRENGTHENER
Slowly lower weight forward, not moving elbow from your side. Repeat 10 times.

TOWEL STRETCH
Pull towel upward but not to the point of discomfort. Hold for 10 seconds. Repeat with other arm.

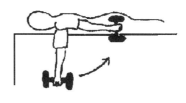

STRENGTHENER II
With hand rotated outward, swing arm straight back. Hold for 2 seconds, then lower slowly. Repeat 10 times.

Motivation Techniques for Lifelong Swimming

8

Goal Setting

Setting goals keeps interest high and leads to improved times.

This statement comes from coaches as well as interviewed Master swimmers. People associated with a team usually work out with a coach, and they are the ones most likely to set goals.

Coaches encourage swimmers to write down specific, realistic goals for the season and work toward achievement of those goals. Serious competitors keep a detailed exercise log book. Included is space for total yardage, type of workout, heart rate, split times and a rating scale (1 to 10) on how the body feels at the beginning and end of the workout. Some swimmers include space for weekly "weigh ins" to see how the body is reacting to workouts. Carolyn Boak of Los Altos Masters and Ann Kay of Rinconada Masters both note that there is a weight loss associated with serious sprint training which provides a clue that these workouts are hard on the body. Log books may be purchased in a sports shop or through swim magazines for a

modest price. You can also make your own chart with a computer and enter times.

There is no set type of a goal. For instance, a swimmer might choose to complete a 100 yards of butterfly without stopping by the end of the season. Or the goal may be to lower your time in the 50 free or 100 free. Some portion of the workout should include practice toward that goal. Seasonal changes mean new goals. Newcomers can use this technique to observe swim progress by modifying the log book to include yardage and time intervals for sets.

The older Masters swimmer is as goal oriented as younger swimmers. Swim times, written down in a log book for future reference, were kept by 90% of interviewed swimmers. It did not matter if the person were 50 or 75 years old. The statement, "that's my best personal time" or "that's my best time this year" was heard across all age groups.

Aldo Da Rosa of Rinconada Masters keeps a daily record of yardage, workout times, chin-ups, balance tests, blood pressure and a scale from 1 to 10 to rate his overall mental, emotional, and physical well being. Marjorie Meyer, The Olympic Club, records each workout which enables her to look back through the year to assess her progress. She can compare her times with the type of workout she has been doing.

Aldo Da Rosa

Dick Bennett of Rinconada Masters is a goal setter. He says that it is important to assess where you are, where you want to be, and then set realistic goals. He had shoulder surgery in 1994. His goal was to swim the 200 yard free in 2:06 in 1996.

One example of goal setting is the following. Several Rinconada Master swimmers formed the "31 club". The purpose of this club was to swim the 50 yard freestyle in 31 seconds or less in competition during 1996. To train toward this goal a portion of one or two workouts per week included doing a set of 5 descending 50 frees on a 2 minute interval. Initially, the starting point was to do the first 50 in 45 seconds, then descend each 50 by at least 2 seconds, arriving at a final 50 in 36 seconds or less. As improvement continued, the first starting time lowered to 40, then 38 seconds.

This type of a goal is fun because it is performed in a group situation. Each swimmer stimulates the next swimmer. Even if the goal is not attained, there has been a purpose and challenge to the workout.

Ray and Zada Taft, former San Mateo Marlin coaches, would agree that this type of goal setting keeps the Master workouts fun. Zada says, "It is important to keep the program fun and reasonably low-key".

Nancy Rideout, Tamalpais Masters, found it difficult to set goals after turning 50. She felt she lost consistency in her workout times. She could not set a realistic goal and feel confident that she would be able to achieve the goal. Some days she would swim fast but other days it was an effort. Many older swimmers can equate with this feeling.

Mike Collins, past Davis Aquatic Masters coach and now part of *Swim Magazine* staff, might have an answer for this common problem. Swimmers get depressed if swim times become slower, but Mike says they need to know this decline is normal. He likes swimmers to try other events to stay motivated and develop new goals. By trying different events and distances new personal times are achieved. For several years, at the beginning of the short course calendar year, I would select one stroke to improve. For the next two months a portion of the workout was geared toward drills and concentrated stroke technique with help from the coach. The concentrated effort usually paid off in lowered times and kept me motivated.

Mike Collins

Stroke Drills

Drills are part of stroke instruction. They are a type of motivation because they encourage swimmers to try to improve. Drills are specific exercises designed to enhance one particular part of a stroke. The advantage of drills is to enable swimmers to feel and concentrate on one area of the body. Swimmers at all levels of proficiency need to be reminded of techniques that promote efficiency through the water. Drills accomplish that purpose.

All the interviewed coaches claim to feel stroke instruction is important. But lack of stroke instruction was a big complaint among interviewed swimmers. I don't know the answer; maybe it is the way stroke instruction is offered. Rick Goeden of Ojai Valley Masters uses an individual approach with an underwater video camera. His swimmers say that when you see yourself underwater you can tell exactly what you are doing with the stroke and that is very helpful.

Mo Chambers, Western Athletic Club Masters coach, incorporates drills into all her workouts. Mo was awarded the Pacific Masters Coach of the Year in 1995 and the United States Masters Coach of the Year in 1996. Her workouts are available to anyone on the Internet at http//www.best.com/~moswimm.

A typical Mo Chambers workout would consist of a warm-up, followed by a drill set, followed by the main set that incorporates the previously practiced drills. It is this pattern of repetition that programs nerve pathways in the brain to perform the correct technique. But it takes time for a permanent change to occur. For example, in order for a physical or behavioral change to occur, the brain must receive repeated stimuli that this new information is important. The more ways that stimuli can be applied, the stronger and quicker the response. Once brain pathways have been stimulated many times, neural connections are reorganized with the corrected motor input. The stroke is now perfect! But, the brain is more adaptable when we are younger. As we age it takes longer with persistent concentration on stroke technique to improve. Does this change take two months, three months or a year? It depends on the continuous effort by the swimmer and the untiring watchful eye of the coach to ensure the new input is correct.

Drills for all four strokes can be found in swim magazines or workout books. Most coaches incorporate drills into each workout. Below is a brief sample of three freestyle drills.

- *Touch and pull.* (hold left arm extended on top of water and don't pull back until right arm comes over the water and touches extended left finger tips. Practice not rushing the arm stroke.) Encourages a long, stretched out stroke.

- *High elbow swim.* (emphasize finger tips pulling up to arm pits, then extend arm forward over top of water. Repeat to other side. By rolling to each side, it will be easier to point elbows to the sky.) Encourages correct entry of hand into the water.

- *One arm pulls.* (keep left arm extended in front or at side and only pull back with right arm for one

length of the pool. Repeat on other side.) Encourages easier concentration on entry and underwater pull of each arm.

MOTIVATION STRATEGIES

At the beginning of each new year, magazine and newspaper articles promote the value of exercise programs as one way to stay healthy. Motivational tips offer ways to get that new person "hooked" into exercise. There are two requirements to stay physically fit. One, the person must be committed to exercise. Two, the person must exercise on a consistent basis. This requires that time for exercise have a high priority in one's life.

Age-group swimmers want social activities as much as workouts to stay motivated. Friends are an important part of a young person's life. Young people need support groups; a place where people care about one another. Team bonding is one reason to stay connected to a team. Coaching requires not only a knowledge of swim technique but the ability to develop a good, wholesome environment where a young person can succeed at his or her own level.

The need to stay connected with a group of people interested in the same activities as yourself continues throughout life. Interviewed Master swimmers rated team bonding as an important reason for staying with a team.

The ability to burn off calories during a workout should be a motivating factor for teenagers, particularly for girls who worry about adding pounds. Swimming promotes long muscles to give the body a firm, lean look. Swimming does burn calories, and as weight training is added more calories are used. Confidence and self-esteem increase among teenagers as the body tones up for lowered times.

But, what keeps a Masters swimmer inspired to work out year after year? Dave Gray of Los Altos Masters says motivation for performance is different for the older swimmer compared to the age-group swimmer. The older swimmer knows there is more to life than just swimming. Usually swimming is juggled between a career, family and community responsibilities, hobbies, and other sports. If the program is not stimulating, there is no one to force that swimmer to stay.

Bill Tingley, coach of Lakeside Masters feels a coach must understand the lifestyles of older swimmers. He wants to know why they are swimming? What do they expect to get out of a Masters program? Then he can design a workout to suit the needs of his swimmers.

I have been asked by nonswimming friends, "How can you stand to swim 4 or 5 times a week? Isn't it boring just going back and forth in a pool for an hour or longer?" I would agree with the boring part if I did lap swimming, but a Master's program can offer diversified workouts, social camaraderie combined with a wonderful sense of mental and physical well-being. I would like to share with you a number of ideas from swimmers and coaches across the United States that encourage motivation.

First of all, any program should be designed to encourage lifelong participation. This means workouts must vary. The variety may be determined by the seasons. Fall is a time to get back in shape after vacations. Winter workouts emphasize stroke efficiency and long distance training for endurance.

Master swimmers may culminate long distance training with team participation in the postal hour swim during the month of January. Notice I said *team* participation. It appears that coaches are needed to encourage swimmers, provide pool time, heat sheets and whatever else it takes to get people involved. Swimmers may participate in the hour swim on an individual basis or as part of a relay. Sprinters are more willing to accept longer distance if there is a goal such as the hour swim. In early spring, emphasis is on shorter distances with a switch toward sprint training to prepare for short course competition in April and May.

Lifelong participation is exemplified by June Krauser who has attended all Master National meets for 23 years and has placed first or second consistently over the years. She and teammate Anne McGuire agree that it is fun to compete and they still look forward to workouts and meets. What are they doing differently from other swimmers? Both ladies competed on swim teams in high school and college. Both are involved in other sports. Anne plays golf most every day and runs 5 miles 4 times a week. June is also an avid golfer. Swimming does not consume their whole life. June was actively involved in the organization of the Master program from its onset. June keeps motivated by designing her own workouts. She lets the coach know what she needs to stay in shape and then does her own thing. Anne follows a set workout provided by a coach but has little input from the coach. Both ladies appear to stay motivated in spite of minimal interaction with a coach. This setup is good for them as they are seasoned swimmers with considerable knowledge and experience behind them. This pattern may not work for the inexperienced swimmer.

Workouts on a weekly basis need to vary. Some teams have a hard workout one day, followed by an easy workout the next day. Coaches expect older swimmers to want an explanation as to why the workout is designed in a specific manner. For instance, a sprinter may want to know why he or she must swim all those 500 sets in the workout. Kids accept a coach's word while older swimmers want to know "why". Swimmers agree that coaches who talk to their people have a more dedicated and happy group of performers.

Fins can be used to provide motivation. If used correctly, they assist swimmers to build up leg, stomach and back muscles, correct stroke imperfections and swim faster with an increase in aerobic capacity. Several swimmers commented that coaches allow fins as a way for older swimmers to keep up with the interval in the "fast workout". I'm not sure this is the best use of fins. To be beneficial, fins should be used for fast kick drills and fast swim repeats, not to make the workout easier.

Rinconada Masters has one day a week set side as "fin day". The entire workout is performed with fins to increase flexibility, cardiovascular capacity and to train the body how it feels to swim fast. There is controversy over the best type of fin to use. Like everything else in our society there is now a choice of several fin types from zoomers (short), scuba type fins (long), to a monofin and so on. *Swim* magazine has published good articles on the advantages of different fin types. Your objective in swimming should determine the fin type.

Swimmers feel team bonding is important to longevity with a program. Motivation to swim is not limited to the water. What goes on outside of the workout is important to individual motivation. Clubs offer a variety of ways to motivate team unity and that special camaraderie which develops from working together for a common goal. A new idea for your club may be found in this next section.

Team Newsletters

Most teams offer a Team Newsletter with interesting information about swimmers, training hints, nutritional information as well as club information and activities. Newsletters foster a connection to the club and to individual swimmers. A sense of belonging encourages lifelong participation. One suggestion was to encourage different members of the club to take turns being the editor.

I would like to share with you an article written for the Water Log, Rinconada Master

Newsletter, dated Jan.–Feb. 1998. The column is called Levinson's Lane by David A. Levinson. Dave usually writes thought-provoking articles for our swimmers. This one reflects the humor that Master swimmers enjoy. This is not the entire content of the article as I left out three book reviews.

Dave says, "It takes more than just working out on a regular basis to become a successful swimmer. You have to get enough sleep, eat right, lift weights, stretch, perfect your stroke mechanics, and learn as much as you can about swimming from published material. Yes, there is an intellectual side to swimming. Unfortunately, many of the best books on swimming remain unread by the vast majority of Master swimmers, possibly because most Master swimmers don't even know these books exist. To remedy this situation, I have listed in this article some outstanding books on swimming I am sure you will find informative."

A Farewell to Arms, by Ernest Hemingway. A comprehensive set of legs-only swimming workouts designed for Master swimmers suffering from shoulder injuries who wish to stay in cardiovascular condition without irritating their shoulders.

Fear of Flying, by Erica Jong. A lengthy treatise on the psychological problems faced by Master swimmers who are afraid to swim the 200 meter butterfly. Despite a preponderance of technical jargon, the book provides much useful information on overcoming the mental barriers that have led to the 200 fly being the least popular event in the Masters program.

Finnegan's Wake, by James Joyce. A biography of the famous Yale University freestyle sprinter of the 1930's, Murray Finnegan, written by his slower teammate who spent four years foundering in the turbulence of Finnegan's powerful flutter kick.

Lord of the Flies, by William Golding. The inspirational story of a beginning Masters swimmer who vows to win all three butterfly events at the Masters Nationals, despite the fact that he has never before swum competitively.

The Old Man and the Sea, by Ernest Hemingway. The complete story of the successful swim of the English Channel by Rinconada Masters swimmer John Selmer at age 50. Contains a tremendous amount of fascinating material on his training, his preparation for the swim, and his actual crossing of the Channel.

In the Heat of the Night, by John Ball. An 853-page autobiographical documentary exploring the psychological trauma suffered at the 1987 Short Course Nationals at Stanford University by a Masters swimmer whose 500 yard freestyle heat was not swum until after 11:00 PM due to the unusually large number of entries in the event.

Turner Diaries, by Andrew MacDonald. The swimming log books of a Masters swimmer who at first was able to do only open turns during freestyle races, but, by practicing one thousand flip turns every day, became famous for having the fastest turns in the USMS.

The Count of Monte Cristo, by Alexandre Dumas. A no-holds-barred exposé of Monte Cristo, a corrupt Arkansas swimming official, who accepted a bribe to alter, from 66 to 64, the length count of a swimmer's 1650 yard freestyle race so that the swimmer could make the NCAA cut. The book documents Cristo's arrest, trial, and conviction for fraud, and chronicles his subsequent meteoric rise to a position of power and influence in the Clinton White House.

I hope the authors of these books enjoy humor as much as I do.

Secret Supporters

Walnut Creek swimmers going to Nationals participate in the following optional exercise. Swimmers who wish sign up to be a secret "pal". Names are drawn at random. Each person on the list is secretly given the name of another swimmer on the list to "support" while at Nationals. The ways in which swimmers are "supported" is varied and at the discretion of the secret supporter. Supporters send greeting cards, balloons, candy, even gifts that are personalized with favorite nicknames etc. to encourage team camaraderie and motivation. Rooms or doors may be decorated with words of encouragement. The secret supporter is never revealed!

Pasta Feed

Multnomah Athletic Club in Oregon offers a "pasta feed" prior to a big team competition. Some clubs use this time to discuss race techniques (visualization, relaxation, focus). This club offers a variety of awards such as "Swimmer of the Year", "who is present the most award", and a visible bulletin board for swim records.

Birthdays

Birthdays appear to be a good excuse for swimmers to indulge in their favorite non-exercise activity - eating. Swimmers commented that they swim to eat what they want! Going out to share a meal with team members after a workout or after a meet is a great way to enjoy the company of others.

Birthday gettogethers are a popular way for swimmers in many clubs to share in the joy of eating and friendship. Rinconada Masters in California posts the birthdays of all swimmers at the beginning of each month on a large, permanent blackboard for all to see. Carol Adams of New England Masters said "swimmers are the only group of people I know who delight in being a year older, especially when the age group changes". It is great to be the "new kid" in the age group.

Awards Party

Besides good food, the best part of this kind of get-together is the silly awards such as: "the best excuse" or "sandbagger", "the best talker on a kick board", "the best lane puller" or awards to those who always arrive late for workout or get out early. Members feel it is important to recognize those swimmers who improve. But it is equally important to recognize all swimmers. I'm sure every club can come up with special awards to fit the diversity of the club members. The top notch swimmers will get their awards at competition meets.

Silent Auction

Fund raisers are necessary to keep teams solvent. A silent auction is an event that not only brings in money but is fun. Many clubs use silent auctions as a way to raise money for club activities.

Fun Meets

Many clubs hold intersquad meets that are not sanctioned and require little administrative time by club members. Time trials or relay meets with nearby teams are a good way for swimmers to see the results of sprint training and meet swimmers other than lane mates. Relay meets decrease the limelight on individual swimmers as everyone contributes equally to the outcome. San Mateo Marlins and Rinconada Masters used to have a 10 man and 10 woman relay team composed of one member of each age group. Several relays could be formed if a team has many participants. Awards were given to the winning teams.

Sanctioned Meets

Sanctioning a meet, either at the local or national level, requires team cooperation. It may be a lot of work to encourage 100% participation but the rewards of team camaraderie are worth the extra labor.

Lavelle Stoinoff, Multnomah Athletic Club

Carol Adams,
new kid in the age group
and Pat Petterson,
New England Masters

Warmup attire by
Clarine Anderson,
Los Altos Masters

History of Masters Swimming in the United States

9

Masters swimming is the newest branch among all the swimming activities. Its history is scattered throughout several sources. One primary resource called *Master Swim History*, compiled by Hamilton and Mildred Anderson, was used the most for reference material. Articles collected over the years provided another source. A third source came from personal discussions with swimmers involved in the organizational process of Masters swimming.

The first Masters Swimming Championships were held May 1, 1970 in Amarillo, Texas, sanctioned by the American Athletic Union better known as AAU but sponsored by the US Coaches Association and the Amarillo Aquatic Club. Actually, the idea for this program began much earlier, between two men interested in the health and fitness of older adults. Captain Ransom J. Arthur, MD coached a group of navy men in the 1960's at a time when the medical field started to link poor health with a lack of adequate exercise. The Navy provided Dr. Arthur with funds to conduct research on this link, using his navy swimmers.

Results indicated that swimming was the best exercise for overall health and, in particular, cardiovascular health. With these data, Dr. Arthur attempted to interest the Amateur Athletic Association in an organized swim program similar to existing track and field programs. He was not successful until he met John Spannuth, President of the American Swimming Coaches Association, during 1968-69. John encouraged him to write a program and offered the use of the Amarillo Aquatic Club facilities where he coached the first meet. This short course meet had age divisions set at 25+, 35+, and 45+. Setting the age limit at 25 would ensure that Masters swimming would not compete with existing national and international competitions. There were no real teams as we know them today. People who were known to be past swim competitors were notified of the meet. There was a shortage of swimmers over 55 years of age. The events offered were 50, 100, 200, and 400 freestyle; 100, 200 backstroke; 100 breast, butterfly and IM. A total of 49 competitors participated by paying $3.00 for an AAU card and showing a doctor's health certificate. A total of 8 events could be swum by each entrant. Winners were awarded plaques as well as high point awards.

The following year, a second short course meet was scheduled at the same Amarillo facilities and again sponsored by John Spannuck and his Aquatic club. This time 112 participants competed. The 200 breast, 50 butterfly, and relays for the age group 25-34 were added to the original list of events.

In October of 1971 at the Fall Aquatic Convention, the Masters swim program became an official part of the AA. An executive committee was formed to determine rules, agendas and the future direction of the Masters program. Teams were formed. Regional meets, short course and long course championships were scheduled. Legality of using either the "frog" or dolphin kick for butterfly was agreed upon. Yearly conventions were scheduled.

Masters swimming, as an organized sport, started in 1972. At this time San Mateo, CA, hosted the short course championships. The age divisions were now five year increments, still starting with 25+ and went up to ages 60-64. The 1650 free was added to the list of events. Participants were allowed to enter as many events as they wished but could only swim 7. That meant a lot of scratched events occurred at the meet, after sizing up the competition. The meet was held over a period of three days. This was the first year to recognize All-American swimmers with a patch and certificate. A new subscription publication, the SWIM-MASTER, was created in 1972 with June Krauser as Editor. It was published 9 times yearly to inform swimmers about meet schedules, results, top-ten swimmers and articles of interest to Masters swimmers.

During 1973, 74 and 75, the number of competitors at championships increased to somewhere between 500 and 600. At the 1973 short course meet in Santa Monica, CA, the relays were changed to 25+, 35+ and 45+ age divisions. Later the 55+ and 65+ age groups were added. The first Masters International Swim meet was held in March of 1974 at Sidney, Australia. Masters swimming was well on its way to increased popularity and approved by the medical community as a way to promote overall health.

By 1976, the number of swim competitors had grown to 800 at the Short Course National Championships in Mission Viejo, CA with 98 teams being represented. The larger number of entrants led to the first scheduled four-day meet to occur at the Long Course Nationals held in St. Louis, MO. This meet hosted 514 contestants from 93 teams. In 1977 the First Postal Masters Relays were organized, sponsored by Hawaii. Masters swimming was growing with age groups added up to the 70 year bracket.

By the end of the 70's, the number of registered Master swimmers had reached 5,000 with the oldest swimmer registered at 88 years of age. Dr. Ransom Arthur continued to be a driving force behind the growing success of the program, providing leadership and research at yearly conventions. Other contributors to the early development of the program were Ted Hart, June Krauser, Buster Crabbe and Doc Councilman.

In 1979, a Congressional Act was passed that forced the AAU to disband and allow any sports team that wished to form its own governing body. The Masters were ready for change but considerable confusion existed as to the relationship of the growing Masters swim program to the existing United States and World governing sport's organizations. Controversy also centered around the definition of an amateur. Where did this program best fit — with FINA, US Aquatics Sports, US Olympic or as an independent group? A decade after the first National Meet in Amarillo, the number of competitors at the Short Course Championships in Ft. Lauderdale, FL and the Long Course Championships in Santa Clara, CA reached 900 plus. Offshoots of the original swim program were postal Master meets, postal relays, the hour swims, open water swims and the popular diving meets. The program was successful, growing, and wanted to stand on its own. In 1980 at the aquatic convention in Snowbird, Utah, representatives to the convention decided that Masters swimming was to be a separate, nonprofit corporate entity, called United States Masters Swimming (USMS). Local swim committees across the United States were formed with officers and bylaws. USMS would be represented by US Aquatic Sports but would have independent rules and regulations. At that point in time, FINA did not support the Masters program.

Over the ensuing years a steady increase continued in the number of swimmers registered with USMS. The work done at the local level by the swim committees and augmented by zone committees increased registered swimmers from 11,881 in 1982 to 14, 899 in 1983 to 15, 591 in 1984 and finally to 25,118 in 1987. On the international level, FINA finally recognized Masters swimming as an independent entity. In 1986, the first FINA World Masters Swimming Championships were held in Japan under FINA rules.

The 1987 National Short Course Master meet held at Stanford, CA hosted the largest group of competitors to date, 2,328 entrants. By this time the 19–24 age group had been added to the existing age groups. The number of events entered at National Meets was down to six with the option by the host team to reduce that number by one. Scoring and awards for National Meets were changed in 1990 to allow participating teams to be placed in large or small team competition, dependent on the number of team entrants at the meet.

Conventions now considered solutions to best handle the large number of swimmers at National meets. At present, swimmers must have qualifying times in three events of their choosing at National Meets. This leaves two or three events that can be swum without qualifying. Suggestions range from tightening cut-off times to extending the number of days spent competing.

In 1996, the number of registered USMC

swimmers reached 30,000 with approximately 450 clubs. Within 25 years of its inception, Masters swimming has become a well-established program, promoting a healthy lifestyle and social camaraderie for many competitors and noncompetitors. At press time for this book, the number of registered swimmers is 33,000.

1952 Olympic Swimmers Reunited at Santa Clara International Meet

Gail Roper, Masayo Azuma, Della Sehorn

Why Should I Join a Masters Team?

10

The motto for Master swimming is fun, fitness and competition. The order is important because it reflects the original purpose of the "founding fathers". Anyone over the age of 19 who can swim and wishes to workout for physical fitness can join a team. Teams throughout the country have different organization and workout styles. Members have a wide range of choices from non-competitive lap swimming to national and international competition.

According to interviews with Master swimmers, physical exercise, weight control, and stress reduction were the main reasons why older swimmers chose a Masters swim team. Socializing at workouts and meets is another reason why Masters swimming is popular. Over and over swimmers said the companionship of other swimmers was a motivating force for keeping them in the program and getting to practice each week. Chuck Wilmore of Virginia Masters quipped, "I'm not sure why I swim except that other swimmers are the nicest people in the world".

Judith Schwartz & Jack Halliday

Interviewed swimmers agreed they work harder in a group situation than they do alone. They are more committed and disciplined. Being more committed means more workouts per week which leads to increased physical conditioning. On the other hand, there is a large population of swimmers who swim alone due to extenuating circumstances. Very few small (15 to 20 swimmers) teams have *daily* coached workouts. Some have a coach, but maybe only once a week. Some of these clubs have more social events than they have workouts. Twelve people chose to swim alone because pool facilities with a team were too far away. Most swimmers expressed the need for stroke critique by a coach. These swimmers rely on *Swim Magazine* for workout ideas or books that provide swim workouts. *Swim Magazine* appears to serve a vital link to many isolated swimmers for workout ideas and ways to improve. The "tear out" swim technique section in this magazine is appreciated by many swimmers.

Being physically fit ranked high with swimmers from all parts of the country as the prime motivator for staying with a swim team. Seventeen out of forty-three swimmers come from a noncompetitive background. Master programs provide new skills that contribute to being more fit. Swimming has taught these people a lot about themselves in terms of accepting a challenge, teaching an "old dog new tricks", goal-setting and learning *how* to be physically fit. This group enjoyed the muscle tone and weight loss that accompanies a program of physical fitness.

It must be noted that approximately fifty percent of those interviewed rank the ability "to eat whatever they want" as a bonus that goes along with workouts. Swimmers like to eat! And they like the companionship of other swimmers while indulging in this activity.

Lifelong quality health is a motivator for many individuals. Swimming is part of a preventative health maintenance program for many people as they climb the ladder in age. Jim Jones of San Diego Swim Masters got back into swimming after a lapse of 41 years because of cardiovascular complications. Even though he was a top-notch competitor in his youth, he ignored swimming in his busy world until the heart refused to be ignored any longer. He realized the value of swimming as a way to keep arteries and veins pumping blood efficiently in and out of the heart. Marian Wolfe, Arizona Masters, started Masters swimming after her husband's first heart attack. She wanted to be physically fit and lessen the chance of a heart attack for herself. Betty Bennett, Lincoln Masters, swims to prevent back problems and keep shoulders flexible. People suffering from asthma have found swimming to be beneficial therapy to increase breathing ability.

Nancy Rideout, Betty Bennett, Arlene Probsting

Some swimmers enter the Masters program for mental therapy from stressful situations. Others join to stay in shape while recuperating from a running or tennis injury. Doctors recommend swimming as therapy since it is a relatively injury-free sport. It is interesting to note injured athlete's conception of swimming upon entering the program and a few weeks later. Initially they assume swimming is not as demanding as their original sport. This opinion changes during the first week of practice when they are not able to keep up with the endurance of a 60 or 70 year old in the same lane. Generally they are "hooked" to swimming for physical fitness by the time they master stroke technique.

Once into a program, swimmers agree the mixture of ages becomes a real plus. Cindy Baxter, coach of Rinconada Masters, says "Older swimmers are a role model for younger swimmers. It is good to mix age groups in the lane for increased enthusiasm." A number of interviewed swimmers agree that the mixture of ages within lanes is a positive force.

Fellow lane mates do not give a handicap to the older swimmer. Older swimmers must earn their "bragging times". Younger swimmers look with a mixture of awe, respect and envy at the endurance and fast swim times that are recorded by many older swimmers. An example of this respect was evidenced during a swim meet in which three gentlemen in the 70 to 74 age group were competing against each other in the same 50 freestyle heat. I was sitting in the bleachers next to a group of five 25 to 30 year old male competitors. One youngster announced, "You guys have to watch this race. These fellows with the white hair will swim the 50 free in 31 seconds." All the young men stood up to watch what they called a spectacular race. One young man commented, "I hope I can swim that fast at age 74." What a nice compliment!

Several swimmers mentioned withdrawal symptoms if they did not swim regularly. A common response to the value of swimming with a team was that workouts set the tone for what happens the rest of the day. These people feel a sense of accomplishment after completing a workout. Carolyn Boak, Los Altos Masters, Ted Wathin, Lakeside Masters, and Malchia Olshan, Ojai Masters, emphasized the *endorphin effect* which is interpreted as just plain feeling good after being in the water! Endorphins are brain chemicals released from cells as exercise is increased. They function to regulate electrical impulses between neurons. As one individual stated, "What is great about swimming is that it does not matter how old you are, what you do for a living or how many children you have. You just have to be able to finish the set."

There are intangible benefits that swimmers may or may not recognize as molding experiences for the way they will interact with other people and life situations. Many experiences occur outside of the workout: in the locker room, sharing a meal, riding back and forth to practice or meets. Staying with a team for any length of time, provides a place to observe how people react as they progress through the journey of everyday living. First hand knowledge is gained on the different ways people handle joys and sorrows, new life and death. Certain people become role models. Younger swimmers on our team comment that they are able to observe 40 to 50 years of aging all at one time. This makes a huge difference in their approach to getting older.

For convenience sake, I will discuss situations that affect women first, then men, and finally both groups. It appears the sexes gain different emotional and physical attributes from contacts with other swimmers. Most of this information comes from conversations with fellow swimmers.

Walk into any women's locker room after a workout and you will hear the chatter of numerous conversations going on at the same time. Women seek and discuss solutions for situations from other women. Locker room talk could put therapists out of business!

Conversations of this type are relevant today because many women do not have the intergenerational family contacts that occurred fifty years ago. And women still are the primary caregivers in a family, always seeking new ways to solve old problems. One example is provided by a younger swimmer who commented on the wealth of knowledge s he has gained on the subject of menopause. By listening to other women, I now know what to expect at each age and the choices I have.

For women, breast cancer has taken on a whole new perspective. Swimmers who have a breast removed become role models.

They have the surgery, get back in the water as soon as possible, experience little depression or side effects and let other women realize it is okay to lose a breast. Information is passed on about the diagnosis, options and treatments. What better way to share the ups and downs of life.

Women more than men outwardly share the pain of divorce or death with fellow swimmers. The ability to help and support people through these ordeals provides emotional stability for all involved. Each person grows as a result of the process. It is a learning experience for each swimmer on the team.

Many women over 40 did not have the opportunity to experience serious sports training or competition while in a school environment. Masters swimming provides a setting for these women to learn how to be more aggressive when necessary and more competitive. For the most part, women are pleased with this new direction in life that extends into the work place and home.

Locker room talk for men takes on a completely different direction. Rarely are personal problems discussed, other than injuries. There is a modest amount of job talk but no solutions are sought. Political and scientific conversations exist depending on who is present. Interviewed men enjoy and feel an emotional uplift from the camaraderie of the locker room talk.

From childhood on, older men have been taught how to compete with one another but not how to compete with females. Masters swimming has presented men with the opportunity to learn how to cooperate with females on a sports-oriented basis. They are able to share their physical attributes and receive input from females.

Both men and women agree that friendships formed with members of the opposite sex are an added plus of belonging to a swim team. Each sex agrees that respect is developed for lane mates and this respect leads to close friendships. Men commented that prior to a Masters team their friends were all men. But women friends now come from swimming and provide a new dimension to their lives. I might add that older females concur that males friends are a new experience for them. There is a lot of togetherness in a lane with 3, 4 or 5 swimmers who all want to do their best. This situation requires cooperation as swimmers must recognize their own strengths and weaknesses.

Personally, I have learned through Masters swimming that it is okay to give a hug to a man going through a "rough day" just as readily as I would to a woman. Swimming has taught me to be a good, caring friend to men; they hurt the same as anyone else.

Physical activity has a positive effect on mental functioning and emotional stability. Aerobic exercise fuels the brain with glucose and oxygen which stimulates mental acuity. Human studies on older individuals who participate in regular aerobic exercise suggests that mental tasks can be performed with improved speed.

Stressful situations tax the body with the release of many chemicals. Aerobic exercise breaks down these chemicals rapidly, lessening their effect on organs. Depression and anxiety are alleviated by the positive effect an aerobic exercise program has on brain activity. Conversation that goes on in the men and women's locker room before and after workouts contributes to emotional stability. It appears that a club provides one type of support group that is important to total health and well-being.

There are a couple of reasons for not joining a Masters swim program. One would be not wanting to take direction from a coach. For some independent people it is difficult to accept the word of a coach as to what it best for their body. These people should check out several different clubs as the style of workout and coaching advice varies considerably. Some coaches interact very little with swimmers or the workout may be written on a board to follow at the swimmer's discretion. If there are several clubs in the area, visit them all before making a decision. Another option for independent swimmers is to workout alone but still belong to a club for the fun of competing on relays. I don't recommend this way as many nonwater-related benefits are missed.

Another common reason is fear—fear that stroke technique will be difficult to master or fear that one's swimming pace will be too slow. These swimmers need to read the section by Kerry O'Brien, head coach of Walnut Creek Masters. A good coach understands these fears. Remember the slower you are when you start a program, the more progress you will see within a few months. Keeping a record of swim times is a good way to see this progress. And keep in mind, many good swimmers started out slow.

Friends

Keeping Warm

Ann Kay and Dick Bennett

Nan Blackledge and John Bricker

Technique and Tips from Masters Swimmers

11

Knowing how to swim strokes efficiently helps one to stay motivated. Swimming requires a knowledge of stroke technique, streamlining, breathing, and a feel for the water. These skills are best explained by a competent coach.

The role of the coach is vital to a happy swimmer. The coach is a role model. A coach not only needs to be able to see what a swimmer is doing wrong but explain the error, and make the correct adjustment. Good interpersonal skills are required for these tasks. Positive words about the swimmer's efforts are appreciated. This section includes sample workouts, and tips from coaches with a large population of older swimmers.

Sample Workouts–Coaches

Kerry O'Brien, Walnut Creek Masters.

Coaches who are visible on deck interacting with swimmers are the best! Don Brown, Walnut Creek Masters, describes his coach Kerry as fitting this category. He is enthusi-

astic, no one on his team is slow, and strong words of encouragement are offered to all swimmers. Maybe this is why he has a team of 320 with a large contingent of swimmers over fifty. Kerry was named USMS Coach of the Year in 1987.

Kerry O'Brien

This is Kerry's 17th year coaching for Walnut Creek. He coached age-group swimmers prior to this position. Kerry also competes for his team. He is always on deck taking splits, reading off times, offering stroke correction as well as words that spur his swimmers to do their best.

Philosophy

New swimmers watch videos of world-class swimmers to observe the "ideal" stroke. In the water each swimmer is observed for variations from the ideal due to mechanics, flexibility and strength. Adjustments for the swimmer is accomplished with drills.

Swimmers are videotaped professionally by TRAC Video, a traveling operation based in Southern California. Kerry reviews each tape with his swimmer.

Regardless of swimming background, Walnut Creek swimmers see an initial improvement in swimming technique and times within 2 to 3 weeks of joining the program. As a result of improved times, they leave the pool feeling good about themselves. This success can be applied to many different avenues of life. Once they are successful, they are "hooked" to Masters swimming. Kerry believes positive feedback from a knowledgeable coach is a reward in itself. Motivation to stay with his team is provided by team lane mates.

Success of the program comes from the mixed ages plus a lot of togetherness in the pool environment and outside of the pool. In the pool, fun workouts composed of relays with mixed age groups add to the camaraderie. Or the relay might be composed of 4 swimmers who must descend times. The winning team is the "best descending team". Or racing sets in which the swimmer sets his or her own goal to offer a new challenge. Outside of the pool, birthdays, parties and club activities provide fellowship. Food feasts are a team bonding activity.

Workouts

All workouts follow a competitive structure although only a portion of the swimmers enter competition. According to Kerry, this type of a workout is best for all-round physical fitness. Workouts are probably more individualized than most teams due to pool size (50 meters) and the availability of one to two other coaches on deck to work with Kerry.

There are 5 workouts per day. Monthly calendars are handed out to swimmers with a description of the workout offered each day of the month. The calendar allows swimmers to decide which workout to choose on the basis of stroke or distance that is offered.

New this year is a stroke workout offered at another city pool on Tuesday nights only. Swimmers sign up ahead of time as a maximum of 14 swimmers can take advantage of this opportunity for individualized practice on different techniques. Turns, starts and stroke technique are offered on different nights. Response has been enthusiastic.

Kerry divides the swimming year into four seasons:

> Preseason (Sept., Oct.). Aimed toward getting the swimmer back into shape after summer vacation. Yardage is usually less during this time.
> Early season (Nov., Jan.). Yardage is

increased. Swimmers are allowed to pick distances (sprint versus long distance). Mid-season (Feb., March). Work on strokes.

End season (April, May, June). Preparation for "big meets", work on specific stroke, includes fine tuning and a taper for those swimmers going into competition. Long-course workouts start for the summer months.

The sample workout below called an individual medley or IM uses all four strokes swum in the order of fly, back, breast and free. Pacing and overall strength are emphasized in this workout session.

Medley Workout by Kerry O'Brien

Table 1:

Set	**Advanced**	**Intermediate**	**Beginner**
1. Warm-up	S–300, K–200, P–200	S–300, K–200, P–200	S–300,K–200,P–200
2. Warm-up	S– 10 x 75	S – 8 x 75	S– 4 x 75
3. Main	4 x (150 IM + 3 x 50 fr)	4 x (125 IM + 3 x 50 fr)	4 x (75 IM + 3 x 50 fr)
4. Recovery	3 x (P–150 fr + 100 kick)	4 x (P–100 fr + 50 kick)	4 x (P–100 fr+50 kick)
5. Mop-up	6 x 50 descend 1–3, 4–6	4 x 50 descend 1–2, 3–4	3 x 50 descend
6. Warm-down	300 yards	200 yards	100 yards

Directions:

1. Warm-up: Moderate swimming to warm-up muscles and introduce all four strokes. The last 100 yards of each is a reverse IM (free, breast, back, fly). Beginners could do the last 100 yards regular IM.

2. Warm-up Set: Consists of alternating drills: one 75 free drill, then one IM drill (omit fr.).

3. Main Set: Four cycles of IM without free followed by a short set of freestyle. The goal of this IM set is to descend your time on the IMs. Intermediates and beginners do a 25 yard fly. On the freestyle swims that follow, hold the fastest interval possible to strengthen your ability to bring it home. Take a short rest between IM and freestyle swims and a long rest between each of the cycles.

4. Recovery Set: Use the pulls as an opportunity to go back and practice freestyle body roll. The kicks can be mixed at your discretion.

5. Mop-up Set: Pick a stroke that needs extra attention and descend times down to an IM split time. (For example, if your ideal IM split time for the 50 breast is 45 seconds, swim the first one at 55, the second one at 50, the third one at 45, on a 1:30 interval).

6. Warm-down: Swim easy to get rid of built-up lactic acid.

Pacing

Pacing means learning how to swim with the use of a pace clock. Reading the clock allows a swimmer to develop a feel for how fast or slow one is swimming. Training this way teaches the brain to sense how fast a 40, 45 or 50 second yard swim feels. A sample set for learning to pace is as follows:

- 4 x 150 free descend - start out slow so that # 4 is the fastest swim.
- 1 and 3 are straight swims.
- 2 and 4 are broken on the 50 for 10 seconds. Subtract rest time from total time.

Stroke Tips

Body balance is emphasized in the execution of all strokes.

Freestyle:

Concentrate more on body roll for a powerful arm pull rather than hand steering. Focus on shoulders and hips moving together for an efficient roll. Perform drills.

Backstroke:

Emphasize body roll with drills as follows:

- Three right arms followed by 3 left arms. Place resting arm at side to focus on rotating that shoulder out of water as other hand pulls.
- For a streamlined stroke the hips must be at the surface. To get hips up, instruct swimmer to drop shoulders and head back.
- For a faster turnover, perform small arm upswings 8"–12" away from torso and bring palm more lateral to body, in a ready position to lift arm for relaxation phase.

Butterfly:

Kerry believes if steps 1 and 2 are executed, anyone can swim fly.

1. Place hands outstretched in front of shoulders ready to enter the water.

2. For the catch pull out and down with palms (palms under and outside elbows) on the same plane as the elbows.

Hands are halfway through the arm stroke at this point, ready to push toward body. These steps require strength and flexibility but now you can swim fly.

From here, the arms continue toward the hips and out of the water for recovery.

The next stage is to time the kick so that it will drive the body forward. Each fly arm cycle should be accompanied by two kicks which serve different functions. The downbeat of the first kick begins just as the hands are about to enter the water. This leg action helps to bring the hips back to a higher position on the surface and provides propulsion until the hands reach the "catch" phase. The upbeat of the kick helps to streamline the body and reduce drag as the hands enter the propulsive phase. The first kick is longer in duration than the second kick.

The second kick is executed as the arms are completing their propulsive phase and beginning a slightly upward movement toward the recovery. The second kick generates propulsion that helps to drive the shoulders forward and upward over the water to assist in recovery.

The butterfly body motion is one of rhythm and continuous roll. In fly, a nod of the chin raises the hips in an undulating motion that begins the first kick. Emphasis should be on allowing the hips to initiate the first kick and refrain from kicking solely from the knees down.

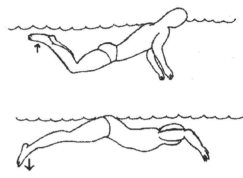

Correct butterfly position

Kerry has the same expectations for all his swimmers, young, middle age and older. He says, "Older swimmers are as serious and enthusiastic as the younger swimmer so treat them the same. Listen to them but don't coddle them".

Cindy Baxter/Carol Macpherson, Rinconada Masters.

Carol and Cindy have been the coaches of Rinconada Masters for 25 years. Carol swam for George Haines at Santa Clara Swim Club as a Hall of Fame National Champion. Cindy received the Ransom Arthur award in 1980 for appreciation of contributions to promote the US Masters Swim Program.

Cindy Baxter and Carol Macpherson

Philosophy

All workouts follow a competitive structure that includes warm-up, drills, sets of different strokes and distances, and warm-down. The opportunity to practice pacing is woven into most workouts with the use of descending sets or straight paced sets (see workout on page). This type of workout provides the best over-all physical conditioning which should be the emphasis of any Masters team. The majority of 150 swimmers on the team are swimming to stay in shape for life.

Although the season may be directed toward Nationals some years, many swimmers take advantage of this training to improve their technique. Training for Nationals includes additional stroke work on technique plus starts and turns. Clinics are offered on visualization, injuries and nutrition. During a Team Effort Meet, there could be over 100 swimmers competing in individual events or relays. This is a time to encourage noncompetitors to get their "feet wet". Swimmers agree that the experience is invaluable!

Both coaches feel older swimmers may have limitations that require stroke adaptations such as breast stroke kick with butterfly arms. They try to accommodate everyone into the program.

The team is big on group support, one reason why it still has many original members. There is a lot of interaction among the ages for events outside of the pool environment: birthday breakfasts, celebrations, Saturday workout that includes a big brunch.

Workouts

There are 11 coach-run workouts offered during the week. Wednesday is "fin day". The workout is designed for fins to improve aerobic capacity (shorter intervals), improve kick flexibility and work on stroke efficiency.

The swim season is planned around these four phases: general endurance, specific endurance, competition, and taper.

General Endurance Phase: 6 weeks (October–November).

The purpose is to build a base of endurance, strength, flexibility, and psychological endurance plus improve technique.

Training is in the form of stroke drills, pulling and kicking, all performed at basic endurance speeds. The amount of fast endurance and sprint training should gradually increase throughout this phase but are not emphasized.

Sixty percent of the weekly mileage should be at the endurance level with twenty percent in the form of intense endurance swimming.

Weight training is encouraged — allowing 3 to 4 weeks to increase size and strength of all the major muscle groups. Build up to additional weights gradually.

Stretching exercises should be done daily — stressing joints of the ankles, lower back and shoulders. Perform 10 to 20 minutes before workout.

Video taping of stroke technique is a valuable method of dissecting strokes with a slow motion by frame VCR.

Snorkels are the newest training method. Since January, 1996, 29 swimmers are using a snorkel for part of each workout to improve lung capacity and work on stroke improvement. The sample workout incorporates the use of a snorkel.

Research indicates the snorkel improves increased CO_2 tolerance, rolling-length-glide per stroke, body position, and correct stroke mechanics.

See Chapter 6 for a more detailed description of snorkel benefits. For most people it is necessary to use a nose clip with the snorkel.

Specific Endurance Phase: 6 weeks (December–January).

Improving endurance is continued but shifting into a more intense level. Emphasis is on specializing in stroke or strokes.

Stretching should continue.

Weight training should shift to fast repetitions designed to produce muscular power.

Sprint training should double at this time. Sprinters should train with less mileage and greater average intensity. They should move into competition phase sooner than athletes who swim longer distances.

*Distance swimmer*s should continue dry land training in favor of swimming more mileage per week.

Psychological training can be performed by visualization techniques and relaxation drills.

Competition Phase: 8 – 10 weeks (February – April).

Most of the important competition occurs at this time. Shift from endurance to race-specific training, anaerobic training and power training with enough endurance mileage to maintain improvements made during the previous two phases. Endurance training is reduced by 10% while sprint training is increased by 10%.

Sprinters: more sprint-assisted training, race-pace swims; increase power training.

Middle-distance and *distance* swimmers: use more short-rest repeats designed to improve both aerobic and anaerobic capacities.

Flexibility and *weights* training both continue.

Psychological training continues but should shift to discussions on conflicts that can interfere with training. Swimmer should practice visualization and relaxation drills.

Stroke mechanics should not be changed after this period. Stroke length and rate should continue so that the pace can be maintained with the least expenditure of energy.

Taper Phase: 2 weeks (May).

This is a period of reduced yardage and intensity to provide the swimmer with an increase in muscular strength. Tapering allows the swimmer to be rested and feel stronger in the water. The result is swim-ming faster with less effort. Tapers vary from swimmer to swimmer. The drop can be gradual OR a drop of 30% yardage may occur in one day. Rinconada uses the gradual approach.

Snorkel Workout by Carol Macpherson.

Warm-up 500 yards.

3 x 200 drills with a snorkel (15 sec. rest between drills).

- 1st 200: alternate 50's– swim with a fist, then regular open hand.
- 2nd 200: catch-up stroke with a 6 beat kick.
- 3rd 200: concentrate on long stroke with a roll.

2 sets kicks (1 set free with a snorkel; 1 set choice with no snorkel).

- 1 x 100 on the 1:45. Alternate 10 kicks on right with bottom arm out front, head turned forward, then rotate to left.
- 2 x 50 on the 1 min. Hands out front, streamline position, eyes down.
- 4 x 25 on the 30. Hands at sides, eyes down 45%, relaxed neck.
- 1 x 50 easy swim.

Main Set (see Table 2):

Table 2:

16 x 100 free select an interval		Advanced	Intermediate	Beginner
fins and snorkel	4 x 100	1:40	1:50	2:00
fins and snorkel	4 x 100	1:30	1:40	1:50
fins only	4 x 100	1:20	1:30	1:40
fins only	4 x 100	1:10	1:20	1:30

(snorkel set cont.)

• 1 x 50 easy swim.

• 3 x 300 pull, freestyle. 1st and 3rd 300, concentrate on roll technique. 2nd 300, no snorkel. 1 x 100 warm-down.

This workout is 3700 yards for the advanced swimmer; intermediates or beginners reduce the main set and one pull set.

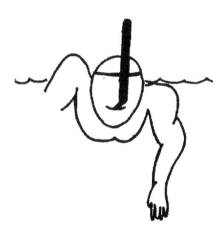

Swimmer with snorkel

•

Ron Marcikic, San Diego Swim Masters.

Betsy Jordan, San Diego Masters, provided the following Main Sets from workouts by her coach of 15 years, Ron Marcikic. Each set reflects a different purpose. In general long course workouts are mid-May through September while short course workouts are the rest of the year. Summer workouts emphasize a lot of freestyle for swimmers who do rough water swims.

Aerobic

Choose an interval for 100 meters (i.e. 1:50 or 2:00).

> 2 x 100
> 2 x 200
> 1 x 400
> 1 x 800

Anaerobic

This set forces one to pace and work hard at end of set.

> Swim a 100, get time.
> Double above time for a 200. Swim 200 and get time.
> Double above time for a 400. Swim 400.

Sprint

4 x 50 — tight interval. Repeat 4 or 5 times with different strokes.

Lactate

Before a big competition do 8 x 100 at top speed. Each 100 followed by a long rest of 8 minutes of recovery while swimming easy laps; take heart rate after each sprint to reach aerobic stage for age.

Many swimmers prefer to swim only their favorite strokes. Carolyn Boak, Los Altos Master swimmer and coach, provided a new idea to me on stroke performance. She feels it is an advantage as one ages to be able to swim all four strokes rather than specializing in, say, free or back. Reasoning behind this statement lies in the fact that there is less stress on shoulders and the back as a swimmer changes muscle groups for each new stroke. Chance of injuries is greater if most of the workout is concentrated on free or backstroke. The same situation would be true of breast or fly except those strokes are rarely performed exclusively by swimmers during workouts. To test this idea, I interviewed injured swimmers on my team and Los Altos Masters. Sure enough, the people with shoulder problems were primarily freestylers or backstrokers.

Jim Miller, Virginia Masters coach and current USMS vice-president, adapts strokes to the older swimmer. He teaches the butterfly with a breast stroke kick for swimmers who have lost flexibility to perform the dolphin kick or for those swimmers who have a strong breast stroke kick. As swimmers age, this stroke requires less oxygen.

Rinconada Masters used to offer a swim clinic for swimmers over forty. The clinic included swim instruction on the double arm backstroke as well as butterfly with a breaststroke kick.

Both of these stroke adaptations are allowed in Master competitive events. Timing of the kick with the arm pull is crucial to efficiency of these two strokes.

Double arm backstroke:

1. Kick off the wall to the flags with a flutter or dolphin kick.

2. Lift both arms in the same manner as in single arm recovery.

3. After arms enter the water, bend elbows toward bottom of pool (hands 6 to 8 inches from surface), keep them close to torso.

4. Direct forearms with palms facing pool bottom toward hips as in single arm power phase.

5. Keep forearms in same plane as elbows; push until thumbs touch hips.

6. Start bringing legs up for inverted breast stroke kick as forearms are pushing to hips. You want power of push to the hips and power of legs closing to occur at the same time. This action propels the body forward and keeps head from going under water.

7. Width of your kick determines when to start the kick. If kick is wide, start earlier than if kick is narrow.

Butterfly with a breaststroke kick:

1. It is best to push off wall with a dolphin kick.

2. Start arm pull. Mechanics are the same as regular dolphin fly.

3. Leg kick is started as arms reach hips.

Power phase of breast stroke kick propels body forward as arms are in recovery phase.

4. When toes are together and extended, arms enter the water to begin the next pull.

5. The kick and arm pull are independent of one another.

6. Breathing can be executed every stroke or every other stroke.

Coaches who can spend time with swimmers receive enthusiastic raves. Malchia Olshan of Ojai Valley Masters says "encouraging instruction will allow one to swim faster and improve technique. The big difference when you swim properly is that you not only swim faster, but use less energy". Carol Adams, New England Masters, echoes the feeling that encouragement is so important. She attended her first International meet in Montreal only 6 months after joining the team because of the enthusiastic encouragement she received.

Malchia Olshan

Master Swimmer's Input

The following information is summarized from the comments of 60 swimmers during interviews. Many swimmers have worked under more than one coach so the comments are not to be reflective of any one particular coach or program. Hopefully, coaches and individuals will look at the remarks as a whole. The comments have been divided into categories for easier reading.

Sprint Training

Lack of sprint training with enough rest was a repeated complaint about coaching and workouts among older swimmers. A high percentage of people interviewed felt coaches do not understand what older sprinters need in order to improve times at a meet. Sprinters want less yardage, long intervals between 50 or 100 repeats and the repeats must be swum FAST!

Carolyn Boak of Los Altos Masters and Ann Kay of Rinconada Masters offer the following input on sprint training. As people age, sprint training is harder on the body than long distance training. It takes longer to recover from a sprint than a 500 event. Therefore, it is essential to train properly for sprints to avoid muscle, tendon, ligament damage that leads to sore joints and permanent injury. Proper training includes a long rest between intervals. For example, 50 yards of freestyle should be swum fast on a two-minute interval. Sprint training should be done at least once a week throughout the year, not just prior to a big meet. The body must be conditioned for hard, fast swimming. Increased muscle

fiber participation and increased oxygen uptake mechanisms are the results of this type of training.

Ann Kay

Marjorie Meyer of the Olympic Club provides confirmation that longer rests during sprint training will not only improve short distance times but also allow for a faster pace during long distance events. Her coach gives a workout that includes 6 sets of freestyle swum fast on the following intervals: 100 yards on the 3 minutes, 50 yards on the 2 minutes and 25 yards on the 1 minute. Marjorie dropped her 1650 yard freestyle time from a 27.15 in 1994 to 26.52 in 1995. Not bad for a 72 year old!

Flavia McBride, Lakeside Masters, was able to improve her times at the Short Course Nationals in Tempe as a result of good sprint training by a coach who understood her goals and provided the right workout to achieve those goals. Rinconada Masters swimmers performed exceptionally well at Tempe as a result of sprint training. A month before Nationals, workouts had to be switched to a smaller pool which meant more people swimming in narrow lanes. The workouts were changed to 25s on the 45 second interval, 50s on the 2 minutes and a few 100 yard distances on the 3 minutes. The competitors were well rested and fast in the water.

Stroke Instruction

Swimmers unanimously want more instruction in stroke technique, including starts, turns and taper technique. They perceive there is too much emphasis on long distance yardage. More stroke technique on butterfly and breaststroke was a common complaint. Older swimmers want to improve and look forward to new challenges. They want the input of a knowledgeable coach. On the other hand, Bill Tingley, Lakeside Masters coach, presented a valid point about coaching. He said, "Some swimmers view the coach as a personal trainer." He emphasized swimmers must understand the coach does not fit this role. It is not always possible to have individual attention when a coach has a large team.

Stroke efficiency is very important as a swimmer ages because there is a natural decline in muscle strength. If an older swimmer wants to maintain a certain speed, he or she must become more proficient at that stroke. There are advantages to learning stroke technique at an early age. Lavelle Sto-

inoff, Multnomah Athletic Club, and Della Sehorn, Los Altos Masters, agree that swimmers who learn stroke technique as a child develop bodies in a special way. Motor pathways are programmed early on. Tendon and ligament development allows for flexible joints. It is not impossible but more difficult and a slower process for an older adult to learn this same stroke technique. Joan Alexander, Walnut Creek Masters, did not start competitive workouts until late in life. It has taken her a long time to become proficient at all strokes and place at National meets. She now feels privileged to be able to compete in the same event with former Olympic swimmers. How well the stroke is performed is more important to these swimmers than how fast the stroke is swum.

Joan Alexander and Donna Monroe

Jae Howell, Walnut Creek Masters, compared Masters swimming to her years as a synchronized swim instructor. In synchro, the instructor watches and remembers each swimmer's performance in a routine.

Immediately after the routine is over, error correction is conveyed to each performer. This immediate feedback is important for perfection. In Masters swimming the feedback may not come until an event is swum in a meet. Jae feels it would be better for the swimmer if the feedback were conveyed continuously throughout workout.

Consensus among swimmers is that more instruction and practice is needed on turn technique. Most clubs wait until a big meet is near to work on this part of swimming. I'm sure every coach has had at least one astonished swimmer disqualified for a one-handed touch in fly or breast. Somehow that swimmer did not get the message in workout. The warm-up period is a good time to concentrate on the correct streamlined form required of a properly executed turn. Gail Roper, swimmer and USF Masters coach, noted that a one-half second improvement in all turns on the 400 IM amounted to a 7.5 second decrease in overall time. Sounds like a good way to lower times.

Practice off the blocks for starts, for most clubs, appears to be confined to weeks before a championship meet. Confidence in starts comes from doing them over and over. The same is true of turns. Interviewed swimmers would like critique throughout the year from coaches on starts and turns to execute them properly.

Taper Technique

The adjustment on yardage prior to competition is called "tapering". Yardage is reduced to give the body a rest. During this period a swimmer should feel energized. When and how to cut back on yardage is a concern of competing swimmers.

According to comments, how to taper is an area that coaches appear to overlook or assume the swimmer already understands. Swimmers who did not compete as youngsters feel unprepared for meet competition in this area. Since everyone on a team does not compete, swimmers who are preparing for a meet want a taper workout and lanes set aside for the taper. Coaches Carol Macpherson of Rinconada Masters and Kerry O'Brien of Walnut Creek Masters agree the tapering process should be explained and started earlier for the older swimmer compared to the younger swimmer. Chances are most older swimmers lack competitive experience at a young age and therefore do not understand the importance of a taper period. The explanation part should convince the swimmer that he or she will not get out of shape with less yardage if they are well conditioned.

Yardage

Clubs with a high percentage of triathletes tend to have long-distance workouts that include a lot of freestyle and high yardage. This type of workout on a daily basis brought the most complaints from older swimmers. The next group of complaints came from clubs with predominately young swimmers and few older swimmers.

Being physically fit is important to all swimmers. In terms of yardage to achieve that goal there was wide discrepancy. Most swimmers workout three to five times a week. About a third of the swimmers put in 1500 – 2000 yards three times a week, with workouts that are considered high quality. And these swimmers place in their respective events. Another third of the swimmers, including Don Brown, average 2000 – 3000 yards, three to five times per week. Don, Walnut Creek Masters, places at the top of his age group every year.

Top female competitors in the 70-74 age group, Grace Altus of Ojai Masters, Jean Merryman of Colonial 1776, and Margery Meyer of The Olympic Club swim 5 times a week, averaging 2200–2500 yards per workout. They consistently place first and second in their events. On the other hand Ray Taft of San Mateo Marlins averages 1800 meters 3 to 4 times a week and younger swimmers can't match his times in some events! Dexter Woodford, O*H*I*O* team, at age 80 swims approximately 1 mile five times a week, and he also walks 2 miles a day.

The highest yardage was reported by Lavelle Stoinoff of Multnomah Athletic Club in Oregon, 5000 yards per workout, six times a week. She consistently places first in her age group in events, especially over 200 yards. She also had shoulder surgery for rotator cuff injury. Are the two connected?

Coaches agree there is a tendency for swimmers to get hung up on yardage. Less yardage will still provide physical conditioning as long as the workout is high quality, which means working out at a fast pace.

Training Routines Of Selected Swimmers

Typical swim workouts, weight programs and stretching routines are given for the following swimmers in their respective age groups. These swimmers were chosen because they consistently swim well in their age group at meets. This information may help you to compare your exercise pattern with other swimmers your approximate age. These routines are what works best for the individual swimmer and are not recommendations for other swimmers.

Nancy Rideout (Age 56)

Sprinter.

Swims 3 to 4 times aweek. Yardage 3000–3500 yards.

Workout:

Warm-up; 10 x 50 drill down and stroke back.

Main Set:

Stretching: (to avoid chronic shoulder problems).

3 sets of the following routine performed twice a day for fifteen minutes. One session is prior to the workout.The other session is sometime during the remainder of the day.

1. Arm circles - forward (30 times); backward (30 times).
2. Each arm brought across body to apex = (30 times each).
3. Hold a streamline stretch position for 30 seconds.
4. Place left hand on right elbow and stretch for 30 seconds.

Reverse arms.

Weights:

> Free and machine weights at a fitness center.
> Trains 3 times a week for 1 1/2 hour sessions.

Betsy Jordan (Age 61)

Backstroke is specialty, middle and long distance preferred.

Swims 2500–3000 yards, 4 to 5 days a week

Does not use paddles—undue shoulder strain.

Uses Zoomers occasionally to increase ankle flexibility and to concentrate on stroke work while moving forward.

Workout:

> 600 —1000 yards warm-up
> Main Set: this one emphasizes drill work.
> Do a 150 drill/kick of free (concentrate on high elbows, long stroke)
> Follow with a 150 free
> Repeat same pattern for back, breast and fly.
> Relaxed 400 kick set by 50's hard, easy; if it's choice, I do back and free.
> 800 pull
> 200 warm-down

Weights: (both free and machine weights — 3 times a week for 45 minutes)

Warm-up with stretching and abdominal exercises; also stretching behind shoulders with a wooden pole.

Perform several sets of pyramid exercises (10 reps at one weight, 8 at a heavier weight, 6 at a yet heavier weight)

example:

> lat machine   (80/90/100 pounds)
> leg extension (80/90/100 pounds)
> bench press   (55/65/75)

Rotator cuff exercise with 5 pd. weights

Triceps lift with 15 pd. weights

Squats with 65 pd. weight

Upright rowing for trapezius muscle, do 12 reps with 2– 12 pd. weights.

Ann Kay (Age 63)

Free and back specialty, sprint to middle-distance swimmer.

Swims 3000 –3500 yards 4 days a week.

Never uses fins (hurts back); does not use a kickboard for same reason.

Uses paddles and pull buoy.

Workout:

500 yard warm-up, part may be backstroke or free drills. Weekly or twice a month includes 5–50 free and breast sprints on a two minute interval.

Main Set: tries to incorporate a lot of drills

3 sets of the following: Reps 1 and 3 are freestyle; rep 2 is choice.The choice stroke is usually backstroke.

> 4 x 25 – alternate drill and stroke - every 30 sec.
> 2 x 50– build on the 1:00
> 1 x 75 medium; rest 5 sec, and sprint 25
> 1 x 100 fast

rest 30 seconds and repeat
Kick Set (always part back)

> 4 x 25 (alternate hands stretched up to sky for backstroke)
> 2 x 50 fast
> 1 x 100— 75 medium, sprint last 25
> 2 x 100 fast

Pulls — 2 x 400 (free and back) no paddles or buoy on backstroke.

10 x 50 or 10 x 25 (no free) always does some fly and works on breast.

Weights:

Does not like weight training but feels it improves swimming.

Trains at YMCA twice a week for 45 minutes.

Uses Cybex equipment—low weight with fast repetitions.

June Krauser (Age 72)

IM specialist, workout includes all strokes. A distance swimmer as well.

Swim 5 to 6 times a week, 3000–3500 yards. Does her own workout independent of coached workouts.

Workout:

Incorporates a lot of drills into the workout.

Backstroke

> 500 yards back drill broken into 50 kicks and 50 swim

Freestyle

> 3 x 200 free pulls with paddles

Butterfly

3 x 200 fly drill down, backstroke back
Breaststroke

> 1 x 200 breast drill
> 8 to 10 fast 50's

Kick for 1000 yards

Weights:

> Uses mechanical weights 3 times a week for 1/2 hour session.

Golf:

> Plays most every day.

Margery Meyer (Age 75)

Long distance, free and back are specialty.

Swims 2400 –3600 yards, minimum of 4 times a week; tries for 5 to 6 times.

Workout:

Always kicks backstroke and uses fins. Never uses paddles.

Main Set: (coach uses a sprint workout for long-distance swimming).

> 30 x 100 free with a 15 second rest. Starts out slow to warm up and keeps going faster - followed by kicking
> OR
> 3 times 400 free for a warm-up
> 12 x 100
> 200 free easy
> 12 x 100 free pace (tries for a 1:35 pace) fin kicks

Does not do weights or stretching.

Marjorie Sharpe (Age 81)

Started out as long distance; now swims all distances.

Swims 2500–3000 yards 3 times a week.

No paddles, no fins, usually no kickboard (due to back injury); uses a pull buoy.

Does not do weights or stretching.

Jean Durston (Age 84)

Middle and long distance.

Swims 2400–3000 yards 4 times a week; no paddles or fins.

Workout:

Warm-up is always a 300 swim, 200 kick and 200 pull. Jean does part of the kick breaststroke.

Warm-up Set:

> 4 x 50 descending set of a stroke

Main Set:

> 500 for time
> 8 x 100 free on the 2:20
> 3 sets of 75 kick and 75 pull (choice stroke)

Likes to warm down with a slow 400 IM

Stretching performed daily:

> AM routine: starts in bed before she gets up.
> on back, alternating knee bends, stretch arms overhead.
> Rest of day–continues stretching exercises throughout the day, whenever she thinks about it.

Ed Cazalet (Age 56)

Middle distances—emphasizes free and back; some IM.

Swims 5000 yards 5 times a week.

Does not use fins or paddles.

Workout:

Warm-up is 500 swim, 200 kick and 300 pull.

Kick is always back (can work on back turn, stay streamlined and no kickboard which is easier on shoulders).

Main Set:

> 16 x 100 - alternate 100 IM on the 1:30 with 100 free on the 1:15
> 10 x 50 kicking (always back)
> 16 x 100 ladder (10 -15 sec. rest between strokes)
> 100 IM
> 200 back
> 300 free
> 400 IM
> 300 free
> 200 back
> 100 IM
> 10 x 50 - alternate hard, easy free on the 50 sec.

Warm-down

Does not do weights or stretching routine.

Jack Halliday (Age 61)

Medium distances—concentrates on back and breast.

No paddles, but uses fins to kick in workout.

Swims 5 times a week, averaging 2500–3500 yards per workout.

The following workout is used to warm up prior to swimming an event at a meet. It takes 45 minutes, about 1400–1500 yards.

> 600 free warm up
> 200 back - medium speed
> 200 breast - medium speed
> To get arms going and heart rate elevated, do 2 x 100 pull (freestyle) on the 2:00, breathe every 3rd stroke.
> 4 x 50 build on the 1:30
> 2 x 50 (fast for 15 meters, slow for the remaining 35 meters)
> 6 starts off the blocks.

Don Brown (Age 64)

Primarily a sprinter but known to swim 400 IM for competition.

Swims 3200–-3700 yards and works out 4 times a week.

Does not use fins.

Workout:

700 yard warm-up, drills, kicks and pulling

Main Set:

> 10 x 100 free – usually on the 1:20. If set is 10 x 50 free, usually on the 0:40. Concentrates on free and back during the main set.

Kick set is fly, back or free.

Pull set is done without paddles (to avoid shoulder problems).

Warm down.

No stretching routine.

Only does weights to rehabilitate from an injury.

Plays tennis twice a week on a regular basis.

Dore Schwab (Age 76)

Sprinter.

Swims 2200–2500 yards 4 to 5 times a week.

Does not use paddles.

Uses Zoomers for kicking.

Premeet Workout:

Warm up:

> 800 yard choice = swim, kick, pull always kicks backstroke
> 4 x 50 build up (start out slow and get faster)
> 1 x 200 kick
> 4 x 24 sprints (choice)
> easy 100

Main Set:

> 200's broken OR 100's broken depending on specialty.

Warm down.

Does not do weights or stretching routine.

Aldo Da Rosa (Age 80)

Breast stroke is specialty but also long distance free.

Does not concentrate on drills.

Swims 3000 yards 6 to 7 times a week

Workout:

500 timed free warm-up (lets him know how he feels that day). Does not use fins.

Main Set: (1to 2 minute rest between sets)

> 500 backstroke

500 free

500 breast

500 free pull with paddles and pull buoy

500 kick– usually breast stroke, occasionally back

5 x 50 fly on the 1:30

Stretching performed daily:

AM routine: (performed in bed)

> Do twice–extend toes and hold for 30 sec. then flex toes for 30 seconds.
>
> Do twice– alternating– touch each knee to chin, hold 30 sec.
>
> Neck stretch to left side, hold for 10 sec., then to right side and hold.

PM routine:

1. breast stroke leg stretch–sit on bent knees with toes flexed; lean forward until head touches ground or close for 30 sec.
2. runners leg stretch (right hand touch left toe then alternate) 20 times each leg.
3. lie on back and bring legs over head 20 times
4. sit on heels while watching TV.
5. stationary bike - 5 minutes with increasing resistance
6. eight chin-ups and 12 push -ups
7. balancing exercise (stand on one foot, timed response)

Weights:

Tries for 2 to 3 times a week, trains at YMCA with Cybex equipment, circuit training.

Jim Triolo (Age 84)

Long distance—freestyle and some backstroke. Swims 4 times a week, about 1 mile.

Does not use paddles or fins.

Workout:

Consists of straight freestyle for 1 mile, occasionally adds some back.

Does not do any kicking.

Walking: walks about 2 miles on alternate swim days.

No weights or stretching routines.

Plays golf occasionally.

No interval training.

Dexter Woodford (Age 83)

Sprints and distance.

Swims 5 days a week, about 1 to 1 1/2 miles.

Workout:

Most of workout is freestyle at the YMCA.

Kicks a 500 to get heart rate up.

Walking: walks 2 miles 5 days a week.

Does not do weights.

Master swimmers are a vivacious, energetic and interesting group of people. Don't let a few gray hairs or wrinkles lead to the conclusion that these swimmers are only interested in fitness. Inside these bodies there is a brain directing muscles to swim down the lane, arms churning, legs kicking up water, with a flip at the turn and an even faster swim back to the finish. The result of this energy spurt is to kick butt and beat that swimmer in the next lane even if it means aching shoulders, backs and knees the next day.

Most Master swimmers have learned the art of play by incorporating fun into some workouts. Mixed stroke relays to celebrate a holiday or the 12 days of Christmas workout may be used to alleviate routine swimming. A challenge among lane mates can be fun if not taken seriously. Women are notorious for talking while using a kickboard. They manage to catch up on news or solve the day's problems. Men either don't enjoy kicking and talking at the same time or haven't figured out how to do both efficiently at the same time.

One of the younger swimmers on my team summed up the aging process with this statement, "After being a Masters swimmer, I now view aging as a totally positive process where previously I saw only the negative factors."

Dick Bennett

This statement does not imply there are no negative factors. The older swimmer learns to adapt as he or she ages. Aches and pains in joints affecting swimmers after age 50 are the most common negative factors. Dick Bennett, Rinconada Masters, calls this process DOS or deterioration on schedule. The way most swimmers approach these "inconveniences" is positive. Do these individuals stop swimming? Are you kidding? If the shoulder is injured, they switch to a stroke that does not aggravate the pain or switch to kick drills. If the back aches, then an open turn is the alternative approach. If the knee is acting up, arm pulls are best prescription. Do they complain? Yes, but they work through the injury and demonstrate that aches and pains can be overcome.

Many aging swimmers develop stretching routines to lessen the decrease in flexibility that is common to older people. Tendons and ligaments become more rigid throughout the aging process, thereby limiting the degree of motion at joints. They are also more susceptible to tears. Stretching reduces the chance for injury. Unfortunately, most people wait until they experience an injury before starting a stretch routine. Chapter 12 contains stretch routines for Master swimmers.

A good example of adaptation is Zada Taft of the San Mateo Marlins. Zada was to compete at the 1995 Long Course Championships in Gresham, Oregon, when her right arm became stiff and sore for unexplained reasons. She could not raise the arm over her head. So, she scratched the freestyle events but swam the 100 back using her

good arm only to earn team points.

As one ages, less oxygen is delivered to big muscle groups such as those in the thighs. At this point, the kick slows down. The swimmer may adapt by switching to longer paced distances and an aerobic workout. The kick can slow from 6 beats to 2 beats, saving the body from going into oxygen debt.

Zada Taft, Lynne Taft De Victoria, Ray Taft

Other swimmers reduce the amount of yardage during a workout. Higher yardage does not necessarily make for a better workout. The quality of the workout is what counts. Doing 2000 to 2500 yards of aerobic, anaerobic training will provide the cardiovascular system and muscles with good training. Follow the intervals and stick to them for a high quality workout.

Swimmers may have to slow down for other reasons. I watched Ray Taft, one of the best Master swimmers in the world, stop 50 meters short on a 200 meter butterfly event because his body could not go any farther. His attitude was, "That's okay, I'll do it another time. This was not my day". His doctor had told him, following by-pass heart surgery, that he would know when to limit his physical exertion. Most Master swimmers have this positive outlook. Remember, attitude is contagious. Is yours worth catching?

Elfriede Rogers, Walnut Creek Masters, is a wonderful example of upbeat attitude in spite of various surgeries. She laughingly calls herself the bionic woman. She has two new hips, double breast mastectomies with reconstructive surgery, and heart ablation to remedy fibrillation. At age 70, she is back in the water, happy to be participating in meets again.

Attitude reminds me of an article I once read that stated nobody grows old by merely living a long time. People grow old when they forget their ideals. Imagine that inside your heart and brain there is a recording chamber. As long as these chambers receive messages of *beauty, hope, faith, cheer* and *courage,* you are young. When the wires in these chambers go down and all that is recorded is pessimism and cynicism, then you have grown old. I wish I knew who wrote these words as I would like to give the person credit for describing Master swimmers.

Beauty to a swimmer may mean looking up at the sky at sunrise or sunset while swimming outdoors and being thankful for the opportunity to view a splendid array of col-

ors. Or beauty may mean the privilege of rubbing elbows with beautiful male or female bodies, as one interviewee so aptly described the workout. All older Master swimmers have *hope*. Hope they will finish the workout; hope they can still breathe after finishing a butterfly set; hope they can out touch that young swimmer in the next lane.

Faith is developed as one learns that the body is capable of performing at high levels of expectation. This statement certainly applies to those swimmers who have experienced serious medical problems. I have personally observed fellow swimmers recover from heart operations, cancer treatments and surgery of all types with record speed. They are back in the water as soon as possible, eventually performing as well or even better than before the medical crisis. Faith is also extended by a coach or fellow swimmer with the words, "I know you can do it". Have you ever watched how older swimmers cheer each other on? They get as excited as any 20 year old. Swimmers encourage and support teammates and fellow swimmers. Notice how cheer is spread from person to person until it becomes infectious.

Courage comes in many forms. It takes courage to get out of a warm bed on a dark, cold wintry morning to swim in an outdoor pool AND even pay for the privilege. It takes courage to get up on the blocks for the first or second time, in front of all those people who are watching, and swim a race you are not sure you will be able to finish. It takes courage to try a new stroke or a flip turn.

Master swimmers carry beauty, hope, faith, cheer and courage outside of the swimming world into the workplace, home and everyday activities.

One day I entered an elevator together with a woman, unknown to me. She commented that I must be a swimmer. My initial thoughts were, "Is my hair still wet or do I smell like chlorine?" I replied, "Yes, I am a swimmer but how did you know?" She said that I had a healthy glow, a happy smile, a lean, mean body, and of course, a tan. Naturally, she made my day! But, I must admit that description fits many Master swimmers.

Carol Adams of New England Masters uses the Masters swim program as one type of role model for positive thinking in her motivational talks to professional groups. She sees swimmers as good role models for goal setting, achievement and just plain having fun as one ages.

Announcing a meet on a cold day.

Above: George Cunningham

Right: Joan Smith

Stroke and Turn Judge

What Aging is All About

13

I am amazed at changes in the understanding of the aging process since the beginning of Masters swimming in the 1970's until the present day. For example, when I joined Rinconada Masters in 1973 there was a 62 year old swimmer on the team, Sylvia Bailey, who I, as well as our coach, thought was the greatest athlete. She swam the 400 IM, the 200 butterfly and the 1650 freestyle in competition and took 1st place in these events. I was impressed a woman that old could manage to swim those distances. I am now 65 years old, swimming faster times than Sylvia, and have to work hard to earn a 1st place. Today, older swimmers are expected to function efficiently at athletic events. As I age, my expectations change. For instance, I am impressed with 82 year old Jean Durston of Walnut Creek Masters who swims the 1650 and 400 IM in the same day with ease and grace. I watch Ellen Tait swim the 500, 200, 100, and 50 free during a two or three day meet at age 87. I want to be able to swim that way when I am 82 or 87 years of age!

Two of the first *biomarkers* or indicators of aging to appear in humans is a change in visual acuity and a decrease in lung capacity. The ability to focus on near objects becomes more difficult between forty to fifty years of age. Protein in the eye lens changes to a more rigid structure, reducing the ability of this structure to accommodate for near and far vision with ease and accuracy. Second, decreased pulmonary function results in the inability to completely blow out "used" air from lungs during the exhalation phase of respiration. This action reduces space for incoming oxygenated air. Again a change in protein is the culprit with a loss of elasticity in air passageways and air sacs.

Let's look at why these changes occur. There are many biological theories proposed to explain the aging process. The physiologist in me finds these explanations interesting. For the layman, read the simplified version. If more detail is desired, read the biological theories. The study of aging athletes is a relatively new area of interest to researchers. Each year statistics change as people astound researchers with new accomplishments.

Simplified Version of Aging

Why does skin wrinkle and sag? Why does hair turn gray? Even though we try hard, muscles cannot pull as hard or as fast in our 60's as in our 30's. It appears body cells are programmed genetically to function slower as one ages. But, how fast that process occurs can vary from one person to another, dependent on several factors.

Research indicates that aging is the result of random changes that occur in normal cell functions. To maintain and keep the body operating efficiently, cell function must adapt constantly. Body cells adapt by response to built-in genetic codes as well as response to environmental factors such as extreme heat, cold, and sun exposure. Other factors that affect cell function are storehouses caused by overuse. But, lack of stressors caused by disuse will also disrupt normal cell function. For the swimmer, aging, to some degree, results in less aerobic capacity, decreased muscle size and strength, slowed muscle contractions and decreased flexibility. Decreased near vision does not cause concern for most swimmers as the black line and crosses painted on pools are large enough to be observed.

All theories of aging have at least four common components. One component is that at some point in the aging process body cells are unable to replace their internal damaged and worn out parts. The second component may be related to the first. DNA (the genetic storehouse) in cells loses the ability to code accurately, thus new proteins are made incorrectly or DNA cannot correct mistakes made during the coding process. Possibly DNA becomes damaged by environmental factors such as excessive UV light or radiation. A third component is that at some point in time cells are programmed to stop reproducing when damaged. The affected organ will deteriorate and die at this point. Cells within various organs reproduce at different rates. Skin cells reproduce every few hours while muscle and liver cells reproduce only when cells are damaged. If muscle cells are damaged constantly due to overuse, they reproduce constantly. The rate of programmed death may be speeded up by this process. The fourth component involves "garbage" that accumulates over time inside the cell due to continuous chemical reactions. "Free radicals" fit this category of garbage. They are harmful molecules that accumulate in the cell from normal chemical reactions. At some point, the cell seems unable to clear this debris and it interferes with the internal machinery. An example of damage to cells by free radicals can be observed in mitochondria. Within every cell, mitochondria use glucose and oxygen to make energy for all body functions. If they are damaged, less energy is available to organs. Cell function becomes less efficient at this point in time. If the organ is the heart, less blood will be pumped. If muscle is affected, contractile ability will diminish. The following diagram of a typical cell presents a visual picture of the aging process.

Biological Theories

One theory, called the biological clock, centers around programmed gene action within the cell. Several questions arise dur-

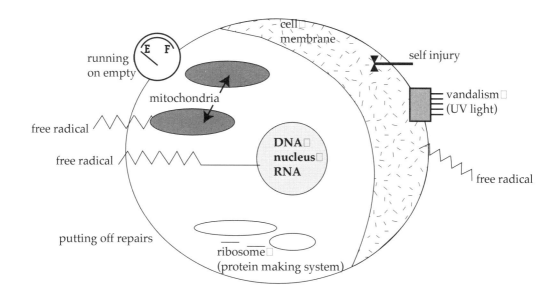

Explanation

Putting off repairs = failure of maintenance system in cell to repair protein.

Running on empty = declining production of hormones or lack of nutrients.

Self Injury = damage to the immune system.

Vandalism = chemical links that weaken, i.e. less elasticity.

Free radical = molecular sparks that cause damage.

ing this process. First, how many times will cells be able to replicate perfect copies of the original cell? As aging occurs, small flaws may appear when DNA replicates itself during cell division. Second, will those flaws be corrected before the end product is finished? Third, what is going on in the cell that allows for eventual deterioration of its machinery?

To answer these questions, we need to look at the role of DNA located within the 46 chromosomes in every body cell. One explanation centers around the end of each chromosome called a telomere. As cells divide, a small portion of this area is normally lost. If a chromosome loses too much of this area due to injury or progressive shortening as the cell divides, a series of detrimental changes occur to the cell. Gene expression is altered, cell machinery malfunctions and cell communication is lost. Eventually, death occurs to the cell when it loses a crucial amount of its telomere. Researchers have studied this terminal section, referred to as a telomeric cap, and determined that it carries no genes. But, it is a vital area to the survival of the chromosome since one of its functions is to prevent chromosomes from shortening during DNA replication.

Germ cells (ova and sperm) contain the machinery to prevent telomeric shortening. Progressive shortening of chromosomes in germ cells would be detrimental to the future human race. Cancer cells never age because they have the ability through an enzyme to reset their telomeric clocks.

Two questions arise. One, how can telomeres in normal cells reset their clocks? Two, do cells that divide more often, shorten their telomeric caps faster? Researchers are working on the first part and have succeeded in a lab environment to re-lengthen the telomeric cap. But, this technique is years away from perfection. Answer to the second questions is yes, loss of telomeres does vary from cell to cell. Cell replacement in organs occurs at different rates. Skin cells reproduce every few hours but muscle, liver, and heart cells divide only when injured while brain cells never divide in the adult. If some cells divide only after injury, then it makes sense to say injuries may hasten the death of cells by faster loss of telom-

eric units. When the telomeres are gone, genetic material is subject to loss with eventual deterioration and death of the cell. It can be said, aging, in part, occurs faster in injured tissue due to loss of telomeric units.

The wear and tear theory is another way of explaining how cells age. Internal and external agents cause damage to cells. UV light is a good example of an external agent that damages DNA in skin cells. Cells have built-in mechanisms to repair damage. For instance, DNA damage can be repaired by special proteins when stimulated through gene action. But, increased damage to the cell can reduce gene efficiency. When this happens, a mutation in DNA occurs. It may take years for the cell to reach this stage. Most of us have experienced diminished gene efficiency to repair sun damage as indicated by changes in skin color (liver spots) or texture (wrinkles).

One example of an internal agent acting on cells is the build-up of free radicals from normal chemical reactions that occur during cell metabolism. A free radical is an unstable molecule capable of reacting with cell membranes to cause permanent damage to cell proteins, lipids, mitochondria and DNA.

An example of free radical formation is to look at what happens in the cell during strenuous exercise. Researchers feel exercise greater than five hours per week may decrease the effectiveness of the immune system due to an increase in free radical production. On the other hand, free radicals in lung tissue may be formed from air pollutants that contain strong oxidizing agents such as nitrogen dioxide or ozone. These oxidative agents are inhaled during exercise. They cause weak bonds in molecules within cells to break. This chemical action leaves oxygen as an unpaired electron (not desirable in the body) or better known as a free radical. When free-radical damage goes unchecked, the part of the body affected begins to age.

Another example of destructive free radical build-up is the damage incurred to mitochondria within a cell. They are attacked by the free radicals, leaving them less efficient to produce energy molecules. Mitochondria are the energy-producing machinery in cells that form ATP (adenosine triphosphate) molecules from glucose and oxygen. All cells require ATP to perform mechanical and chemical processes. Muscle cells manufacture and require huge amounts of ATP to perform efficiently. A single muscle cell requires hundreds of mitochondria churning out ATP to sustain the body through a single workout.

Scientists theorize that antioxidants such a Vitamins A, C and E discourage the destructive effect of free radicals. Vitamin E on the surface of lung tissue reacts with free radicals, preventing them from reaching underlying cells where they can do damage. On the other hand, Vitamin C strengthens collagen (protein) in and around all cells, thus lessening potential damage by free radicals. Vitamins A, C, and E also strengthen cells of the immune system which repair damage caused by free radicals. So, eat your veggies and fruit every day, because they contain these vitamins!

What to Expect From the Aging Process

The human body consists of several systems and levels of structural organization that interact with one another in various ways. Only body parts concerned with strength or oxygen delivery will be discussed here as they are the systems most directly involved with swim performance. How to offset this natural aging process is interspersed through the chapter.

Aging proceeds at different rates within body organs. For the athlete, the condition of the heart and blood vessels is vital to performance. The ability to move oxygen quickly to muscle cells is a key to athletic efficiency. In the absence of coronary artery disease, the aging heart maintains stable function except for one area. During exercise, particularly sprints, there is a decrease in the maximum attainable heart rate. In other words, the maximum heart rate at age 25 may be 190 - 200 beats per minute while at age 75 that same maximum rate decreases to 150 beats per minute. This action may be due, in part, to the heart's decreased response to the hormones norepinephrine and epinephrine which are released during times of stress. It may also be due to a decrease in the availability of oxygenated blood. There is also a longer recovery rate needed for the heart to return to near normal beats per minute as one ages.

What all this means to the aging athlete is, during times of stress, the heart cannot increase cardiac output (blood volume pumped out of the heart into vessels) as efficiently as when younger. Consequently, muscles will not receive oxygen quickly and muscle performance will be slower. Examples are provided by input from Michael Collins, coach of Davis Aquatic Masters and Kerry O'Brien of Walnut Creek Masters who concur that one reason older swimmers start doing longer distances and less sprints is that the kick goes first as one ages. This makes sense if you look at the muscles needed for a strong kick and the amount of oxygen required by these muscle groups to perform efficiently. If oxygen transfer mechanisms in the body decrease with aging, then large muscle groups such as the quadriceps and hamstrings in the thigh region will not contract as vigorously.

Coaches who have large numbers of older swimmers agree that it is necessary to concentrate on forcing the circulatory system to deliver oxygen as quickly as possible by working the kick sets hard, then long rest and kick hard again. Fins used at least once a week will help achieve this goal. The cardiovascular system responds favorably to increased exercise. The elastic fiber in blood vessels maintains flexibility and increased diameter. Heart muscle chambers increase in size to hold and expel more blood.

Are you a swimmer who uses the kick set to rest or talk? If you are, take advice from Yoshi Oyakawa of Buckeye Masters who brought his 100 backstroke time down by concentrating on more fast kick drills in workout.

Elastic fiber throughout body tissues is subject to change with aging. The greatest change is observed in the protein that makes up the fiber. In general, elastic fibers become less pliable with age. One example is noted in arterial blood vessel walls that will be more rigid as elasticity decreases. The heart has to work harder to push blood through rigid walls compared to elastic walls which is evidenced by a rise in diastolic blood pressure (lower number) and eventually the systolic blood pressure (top number). Because all organs depend on the circulatory system for nutrients and oxygen, degeneration causes widespread effects to other systems. To slow down the loss of elasticity, work the cardiovascular system as hard as possible. Elastic fibers respond favorably to constant stretch by remaining more flexible. For the swimmer, this means kick hard and fast; swim as fast as you can for a portion of each workout.

Overall, muscle mass begins to decrease as cell reproduction slows during the aging process. This factor is also responsible for loss in muscle performance. Is there a way to improve muscle efficiency in spite of aging factors? An interesting study conducted by Washington University in St. Louis compared eight well-trained runners, ages 55 to 72, to a group of eight matched runners, ages 22 to 31. Both groups normally ran in 10 kilometer races, consistently placing in the top 10% of their age group. Both groups were comparable in speed and training. The older group had 11% lower maximum oxygen consumption, lower maximum heart rate, and lower percentage of lean body mass (muscle and bone). With these data in mind, the older group should not have been able to compete at the level of the younger group, but they did. Why? Muscle biopsies of both groups provided the answer. The older runner's muscle tissue had less of an enzyme that is involved in the production of lactic acid. Their muscles were less likely to fatigue compared to the younger group. Two other enzymes involved in the burning of fat during exercise were more active in the older group. Larger slow-twitch fibers were found in the muscle tissue samples of the older group which probably comes from years of training and indicates a better ability to perform aerobically. Another interesting side light to this study is that young elite runners who perform much faster than either of the above groups also had these same muscle biopsy results. It appears that early training as well as long-time training results in metabolic changes within the cell to make it more efficient. A good reason why Master swim programs should be designed to encourage lifelong participation.

Another way to improve muscle efficiency is through the use of weights. Recent studies on weight training have shown that muscle mass may be increased, within limits, at any age. Low weights with several sets of repetitions under the guidance of a qualified instructor will increase muscle strength and flexibility. Correct body position while executing weight training exercises is essential to prevent injury. Loss of bone mass may also be slowed or prevented with weight training. To the older swimmer this means that as one ages, long-distance training, weight training plus emphasis on stroke efficiency may compensate for aging factors.

Maximum bone mass is essential to a strong skeletal structure that can sustain the muscular system. Some loss of bone mass occurs during aging and is of concern to the athlete. The mineral content of bones is reduced as the blood level of sex hormones decreases. This situation affects women earlier than men. Bone is a reservoir for calcium and phosphorus. Bone is in a continuous process of mineral deposition followed by mineral resorption for body use. During youth, deposition of bone exceeds resorption, resulting in strong, high bone mass. After age 45-50, the pendulum swings and resorption may exceed deposition, particularly if dietary calcium intake is low. This action will result in bone loss with structural weakness. The deposition of bone responds to stressors. Weight-bearing exercises provide this stress and help to slow bone resorption. Unfortunately, swimming does not fit this category so weight-bearing exercises such as running or weight training are excellent ways to retard bone loss.

For the aging swimmer, the need for more rest between intervals is universal. Lungs in older swimmers tend to retain more carbon dioxide after exhalation which reduces the space for incoming oxygen molecules. The reason for this shift is due to decreased elasticity from a change in protein structure or possibly damage by external factors (pollution, smoking, asthma).

Swimmers need lungs that can quickly exchange air high in carbon dioxide for air that is rich in oxygen. Air moves from the mouth through the trachea, through the bronchial tubes to microscopic air sacs (alveoli) within the lungs. Total lung volume remains fairly constant throughout life. Vital lung capacity (maximum air inhaled and exhaled) decreases with age partially due to less pliable elastic fibers within smooth muscle in the bronchial tubes as well as within the elastic walls of alveoli. Increased resistance builds up which results in increased carbon dioxide-rich air remaining in alveoli rather than being squeezed out of alveoli and bronchial tubes during exhalation. This means there is less space in lungs to hold highly oxygenated air during the next inspiration phase. There is a 10 to 20% decrease in vital lung capacity of a 70 year old compared to a 25 year old person. One way to compensate for this natural loss of function is to concentrate on forcing air out of lungs after each breath while swimming, especially during competition.

One Russian coach has high school swimmers use a snorkel (tube) during workouts to increase lung efficiency. It is possible this technique might also work with aging swimmers.

Oleg Soloviev, former Russian coach, now living in the United States and coaching for Staten Island Aquatics Corporation describes his research with high school swimmers in the *American Swimming Magazine*, April/May 1993. His swimmers have increased lung efficiency 15-20% with use

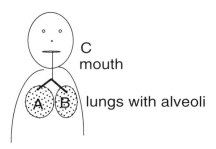

Figure 1

of a breathing tube. See Figure 1 and 2. Figure 1 indicates the length of the respiratory tract as C (mouth) to lungs (A and B). Figure 2 is equivalent to having a longer respiratory tract when the tube is inserted in the mouth. The lungs are forced to work harder to push air out the increased distance from C to D provided by the tube. If used on a regular basis, Soloviev claims the lungs work more intensely and become more powerful. This statement makes sense since it is known that elastic fibers in tissue respond favorably to being stretched by deteriorating at a slower rate.

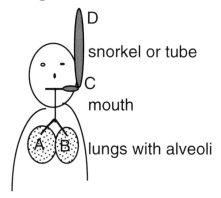

Figure 2

Starting in January 1996, 27 swimmers on the Rinconada Masters Swim Team, ages 29 to 78, used the snorkel for part of each workout. I tested these swimmers to determine if older swimmers could increase pulmonary volume. Each swimmer's vital lung capacity was pretested, then tested again at 3 months and at 1 year. Records were kept on each swimmer's total yardage using the snorkel. It appears there is a small increase in lung capacity if the swimmer used the snorkel consistently at least 3 times a week for approximately 1000 yards per workout. As one 70 year old participant said, "Any increase at my age is a plus, even if it is a small one." The increase was greatest at 3 months when interest in the snorkel was high, and dropped at 12 months as some swimmers decreased their total yardage use with the snorkel. Discussions with a medical doctor led to the conclusion that the increase in pulmonary volume was due to stronger respiratory muscles which allowed for greater chest expansion. If you wish to read the detailed version of this study, it was published in *American Swimming Magazine*, Volume 1997/Issue 5.

Added benefits to the swimmers were realized from this study. Swimmers felt snorkel use could improve body position and stroke mechanics.

If used properly, the head is stationary during snorkel use. This position allows the swimmer to concentrate on arm entry and path of arm pull to improve the stroke. Prolonged use of the tube should stimulate the brain to provide new pathways for the corrected stroke. When the swimmer is not using the tube, the corrected motion will be continued.

The tube also changes body position, due to head position, allowing the hips to ride higher in the water. For swimmers with an inefficient kick, this new head and hip position produces a streamlined effect. Stretch arms in front with the tube held between the arms. Practice kicks in this manner and feel the water as it flows past the body. Try to achieve this same feel without the tube while kicking.

Joints are another body part affected by aging. A small amount of elastic fiber is found within dense connective tissue that forms ligaments which hold bone to bone at joints. Aging results in less flexibility within joints partially due to changes in ligament elasticity. Injury may also change the quality of ligament elasticity and strength. Overstretch to ligaments can result in increased loss of elasticity, thereby limiting joint movement. Coaches and physiologists agree that warming up slowly reduces this type of injury.

Dr. Walter Bortz, a leading authority on aging at Stanford Medical Center, has studied the activity patterns of primitive man and woman to conclude that our ancestors lived very active but short lives. The active part was out of necessity to survive. The short part was due to disease or severe injuries. Bortz refers to the Disuse Syndrome as being responsible for premature aging of the cardiovascular, muscular, and skeletal systems. There is a narrow region between overuse which can lead to injury and disuse which can lead to deterioration. Overuse of shoulder or knee joints may lead to arthritic conditions but disuse leads to deterioration of ligaments, joint capsule and flexibility. With disuse metabolism slows, muscle mass decreases, bone loss increases, vital lung capacity decreases, and blood clots increase as metabolism and circulation slow down. The conclusion is that body parts were designed to be used in moderation. Unfortunately for some individuals, genetics may determine what is moderation.

Aldo Da Rosa claims the narrow margin between overuse and disuse shrinks with age. For him, at age 77 and 3 months it disappeared and any use became overuse and underuse simultaneously. For Dore Schwab, Tamalpais Masters, the decline in body efficiency came earlier, about 67 years.

The point is that most of us will experience injuries, surgery or major illness throughout our lifetime. How we recover from these intrusions on our body depends a great deal on the amount and quality of physical activity in our lives. Swimming has many advantages over other sports as one form of physical therapy. It is gentle on body parts, encourages three-way flexibility of shoulder, knee and hip joints, promotes increased circulation of blood through accelerated heart action and encourages a good appetite. A Master swim program provides the social interaction which is part of mental therapy needed for fast recovery.

Rinconada Swimmers, ages 55 to 83, at FINA Meet, Montreal

l–r. Ann Kay, Dick Bennett, Bobbie Callison, Aldo Da Rosa,
    Carol Macpherson, Ellen Tait

Self Tests to Evaluate Your Aging Rate

14

As a participant at swim competitions, I have observed that Ray Taft of the San Mateo Marlins and Aldo Da Rosa of Rinconada Masters, both in the 75–79 age group, swim as fast as many fifty year old men. Obviously their chronological age and biological age are not the same. How do these two figures compare and what can these men expect in the future? Research is attempting to answer such questions.

Dr. Roy Walford at the School of Medicine, University of California, Los Angeles, has written two good books on aging. One of the books, *The 120 Year Diet* provides ways to determine biologic age. He refers to biomarkers as indicators of functional age not chronological age. A biomarker is a test to gauge the rate of aging on body parts. Some biomarkers such as Glucose Tolerance Test, Creatinine Clearance Test and Lipid Blood Profile need to be performed by medical personnel.

Other biomarkers can be self-tested if you have the right equipment. These tests include systolic blood pressure and vital lung capacity. Blood pressure requires the use of a blood pressure cuff. The newer type with a digital readout is easy to use and does not require any medical knowledge. Take blood pressure at the same time each day over a few weeks to determine an average reading. It is normal for blood pressure to vary throughout the day. I would recommend taking blood pressure first thing in the morning before factors such as eating or working affect the reading. A typical blood pressure reading might look like this: 120 / 80. The systolic reading (upper or first number) is an indicator of the force of pumping action of oxygenated blood from the left ventricle of the heart. Generally this figure rises with advancing age which means cardiac muscle must work harder and faster to expel blood as one ages. The following chart indicates average values for three different age groups taken from Dr. Walford's book.

Table 3:

Systolic blood pressure test	Age Groups		
	20–30	40–50	60–70
men	130	138	140 mm Hg
women	120	136	155 mm Hg

The diastolic reading (lower or second number) is an indicator of the force of the blood against arterial walls during ventricular relaxation. A number over 90 mm Hg indicates increasing resistance in arterial walls due to many causes ranging from rigid walls to plaque (fatty) build-up.

Vital lung capacity requires the use of a spirometer. Hand-held spirometers are available through medical supply companies. These instruments measure the maximum amount of air inspired and expired. The readout is an indicator of elastic contractility of the air sacs and respiratory passageways to take in oxygenated air during inspiration and squeeze out deoxygenated air during expiration. For a sample of normal values, refer to E. A. Gaensler and G. W. Wright, *Archives of Environmental Health*, **12(Feb.)**: 146–189 (1966). The reading is in milliliters of air, dependent on age and height.

Other tests may be performed on oneself without any equipment. These tests include static balance, visual acuity, and skin elasticity. Loss of balance may be another sign or biomarker of aging. This test is designed to determine how long you can stand on one leg with eyes closed before falling over.

Try the following: if you are right-handed, use left leg, left-handed people use right leg. Perform test either barefooted or wear an ordinary low-heeled shoe and stand on a hard surface (not a rug). Stand with both feet together, close eyes, lift one foot 6 inches off the floor and bend the knee at a 45 degree angle across the other leg. Don't move or jiggle the foot. Use a stop watch to time how many seconds you can stand with eyes closed before falling over. Do the test three times to get an average. See chart on the next page for values.

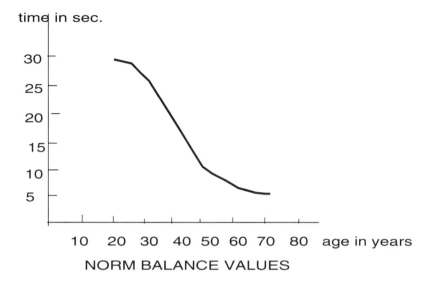

NORM BALANCE VALUES

According to this chart, a 70 year old can stand on one leg for 4 seconds while a 50 year old person may last 9 seconds. Perform this test every other day for a few weeks to see if the time value can be increased. Dr. Walter Bortz of Stanford Medical Center on Aging found that people can improve balance with practice. Exercises such as this balance test, plus weight training, dance, tai chi all increase the receptors and motor pathways involved with balance.

I found that my balance improved substantially after one week of practice, but it deteriorated quickly back to the original time when I stopped for two weeks. The saying "if you don't use it, you will lose it" certainly applies. Sally Scholer, Rinconada Master swimmer and runner, practises balancing after jogging. At age 73, Sally walks forward and then backward on the raised curbing for approximately five minutes after each run. Try it sometime. It was easy as a youngster but not so easy as one ages.

Sally Scholer

Visual acuity tests the ability of eye structures to accommodate from far vision to near vision. Most of us "oldies" know that about age 40, the printed article must be held farther out to see clearly. The next step is a magnifying lens in glasses. To find where you fit in this aging process, select a normal sized printed article in a magazine or newspaper. Hold the article at arms length and slowly bring toward the body. Determine in inches the point at which vision first blurs while reading the print. Compare results to the norm for your age group.

Table 4:

Age Groups		
20–30	40–50	60–70
4.5	12	39 inches

Unfortunately, I've never heard of a way to improve this aspect of aging.

Skin elasticity tests indicate the deterioration of fibers within connective tissue located under the surface skin cells. Connective tissue contains elastic fibers and collagen. Overexposure to sun, wind and cold damages both collagen and elastic fibers in this tissue. As elastic fibers are damaged, they become less pliable and skin loses its ability to snap back when stretched. There also may be loss of fat tissue in this area with aging.

To do this test, pull on the skin with thumb and forefinger on the back of the hand and hold for 5 seconds. Then time how long it takes for the skin to flatten back to original shape. Below are normal values for three different age groups.

Table 5:

Age Group		
20–30	40–50	60–70
0-1	2	15 seconds

For more information on these tests, read *The 120 Year Diet – How to Double Your Vital Years* by Dr. Roy L. Walford, 1988. For information on aging in general, read his other book *Maximum Life Span*, 1983.

Conclusion is that aging is unavoidable. How we age is another matter. For most of us, the quality of life becomes more important as we reach our 50th, 60th, 70th and 80th birthdays. Once an exercise program is started, don't stop because body cell metabolism will deteriorate at a fast rate. It is never too late to add a new exercise, such as weight training or stretch cords, under guided supervision. Body cells will respond in a positive manner to improve the quality of life.

Interviews With Swimmers

Appendix A.

Interviewed swimmers and coaches supplied considerable information for this book. Information was collected between 1994 and 1996. Interviews were held with swimmers from different geographic locations across the United States to get a feel for regional differences that may exist among clubs. Sixty swimmers and coaches from twenty-seven Master teams provided most of the information. I organized comments into a logical pattern. Limited information came from participants in swim clinics for the older swimmer that Rinconada Masters has sponsored for the last four years. Swim coaches were interviewed at length for coaching expertise.

Discussions with colleagues led to the conclusion that somewhere after age 50, aging factors begin to affect athletic performance which separates these swimmers into an older classification. Comments by fellow swimmers in the section on Masters swimming are from interviews with the over fifty group and reflect opinions of that age category. Since most everyone will reach age 50 at some point, the issues discussed should apply to young and old alike.

Parts of the book on aging theories, diet as it relates to physical fitness, and motivation techniques come from my background in physiology and education.

I feel lucky to have had the opportunity to interview wonderful and interesting people from all over the world. I cherish new contacts that I made and look forward to seeing these swimmers and coaches again at future meets. I hope I interpreted people's comments in the original context. Trying to carry on conversations with a loud-speaker blaring in an indoor pool environment is not an easy chore. At the end of a day, my notes were soggy from wet hands, wet bathing suits and water splashes.

INTERVIEW PROCESS.

The general information asked of all swimmers over the age of 50 included:

• personal information (name, age, club, past competitor),

- when and why they joined a Masters program,

- workout description,

- yardage per week,

- workout and pool availability,

- what they liked or did not like about the workouts,

- what keeps them in a Masters program,

- use of weight training or other type of cross training,

- club incentives or motivators,

- cost of swim program.

Swimmers interviewed were members of the following 27 United States Masters swim teams, listed in alphabetical order.

Arizona Masters	Arizona
Buckeye Masters	Ohio
Colonial 1776	Pennsylvania/ New Jersey
Gold Coast Masters	Florida
Holmes JAX	Florida
Jersey Masters	New Jersey
Lakeside Masters	Kentucky
Lincoln Masters	Illinois
Los Altos Masters	California
MOVY - Wichita	Kansas
Multnomah Athletic Club	Oregon
New England Masters	Connecticut
Michigan Masters	Illinois
O*H* I*O*	Ohio
Ojai/Santa Barbara	California
OKMS	Oklahoma
Rinconada Masters	California

Rocky Mountain Masters	Colorado
Sacramento Masters	California
San Diego Swim Masters	California
San Mateo Marlins	California
Santa Clara Masters	California
Stanford Masters	California
Tamalpais Masters	California
The Olympic Club	California
Virginia Masters	Virginia
Walnut Creek Masters	California

SUMMARY OF SWIM PROGRAMS OUTSIDE THE UNITED STATES.

Swimmers and coaches were interviewed from the following countries during the V World Games in Montreal sponsored by FINA — Australia, Brazil, Canada, France, Germany, Great Britain, Israel, Italy, Japan, New Zealand, South Africa, and Switzerland. Intent of the interviews was to compare world-wide swim programs available to the older Master swimmer.

The largest number of competitors at the World Games came from Japan and Canada. Japan had 191 different clubs with a total of 464 swimmers while Canada had 153 clubs represented but 1,187 competitors attended.

Australia

Pool availability is high with both 25 yard and 50 meter pools open to Master swimmers. Coaching varies, depending on the club. In Queensland which has the second largest club in Australia, the coach's job is voluntary. Therefore coaches do not stay long so there is constant turnover in coaching quality. Not a desirable situation.

Weight training is available and recommended to swimmers. Clubs in Australia are very social with a lot of activities offered beside swimming.

Brazil

Enthusiasm and team camaraderie is the outstanding feature of Brazilian teams. These swimmers cheered the loudest for their teammates. Most of their swimmers were under fifty.

Outstanding older swimmer representing this country is Maria Lenk who competed in the 1932 and 36 Olympics. Although Brazil has many pool facilities, coached teams and health clubs, she prefers to work out alone.

Most swimmers participate in another sport and have access to weight training programs. Physical fitness appears to be important in Brazil.

Canada

Swimmers from Canada have access to many pool facilities and coached workouts. Linda Brett, Toronto, Canada, at age 44 is the oldest swimmer on her team. Workouts at her club are individualized with stroke instruction, drills and intervals.

Kay Easun also from Toronto, but with a different club, has been a coach and is now competing. She does not want to see time standards set for Master meets as it would limit the joy of competition for the slow swimmer. She contends that coaches need to flexible and willing to meet the needs and disabilities of the older swimmer.

France

It is difficult for the serious Masters competitor to find pool facilities for coached workouts. Adults are not encouraged to train. Coached workouts are mainly for youngsters. Adults use private clubs to swim but must provide their own workout. They also swim with people who are not part of a Masters team.

Germany

Coached workouts are offered for all ages; even private clubs have coached workouts for adults. Workouts are varied with interval training and time intervals adjusted to the older adult swimmer. Adults are encouraged to swim and train. A trio of ladies, age 56 to 80, enjoy the social aspect of Masters swimming as much as the competition. Cross training such as cycling and weight training is available and encouraged.

Great Britain

Pool facilities are lacking. There are only eight 50 meter pools in all of Great Britain. There are Master teams in Liverpool and London. Many pools lack lane lines or have limited hours or no coaches.

Master swimmers, Jane Asher and Flora Connolley, put in very little yardage compared to US swimmers but perform exceedingly well in competition. Jane swims in several different pools, trying to get enough yardage for swim efficiency and coaches on the side. Flora swims at a physical fitness center in Scotland. Jane does a lot of one arm drills, fly kick underwater and no backstroke due to pool conditions that are shared with noncompetitive swimmers.

Israel

Edith Thein was the only competitor from this country, swimming for Arad Masters. Although Israel has had a Masters Association for the past two years, Edith's husband coaches her in her specialty, backstroke. She was a past competitor for Czechoslovakia and swam in the Jewish Olympics last year.

Italy

Renata Marting has a son who was an Olympic swimmer and she started the Swimming Federation program in Italy 10 years ago. Adult swimming is encouraged and there are good pool facilities available. This program has attracted many adult swimmers with 18 to 20 meets per year. In fact, 1,000 swimmers may attend one meet which means each person is limited to two events. Awards and prizes are given at the end of the year for accomplishments.

Japan

Japan was also well represented in 1995 at the Santa Clara International Meet in California with 45 competitors. Fifteen of these swimmers were over 50 with the oldest swimmer at 68 years of age. Masayo Azuma, 60 years of age, set world records in the 100 and 200 meter breaststroke. She competed in the 1952 Olympics as a breaststroker. Many of Japan's clubs and pool facilities are located near Tokyo.

Japanese culture encourages swimming as a form of physical fitness for older adults. There are many 25 and 50 meter pools available to swimmers. The coaches I met were young and enthusiastic. Workouts averaged around 2000 meters, 3 times a week— not too much different from workouts offered in the United States.

New Zealand

Northland Masters has one indoor pool and access to several outdoor pools which need a cover for year-round swimming. Workouts are coached with both distance and sprint training, and underwater video taping.

South Africa

In the summer, outdoor heated 33 yard pools are available for Gloria Williamson while in winter she has access to an indoor pool. There are coached workouts, although she prefers to swim on her own with workouts provided by a friend. She swims for health and recreation.

Switzerland

Uta Schneider was the only competitor from this country. She has access to both a 25 and 50 meter pool with coached workouts, although she prefers to workout at a private swim club. Normally swims 6 to 7 times a week and enjoys the social part of swimming.

SWIMMER PROFILES: Individual Swimmers from the United States.

Master teams are listed alphabetically. Age of the swimmer in parentheses.

ARIZONA MASTERS

Composed of many teams. At national meets they swim together as a state team. At local meets one team may swim against another team.

Edie (65) and Dan (64) Gruender

Edie started the Arizona Masters program in her backyard pool in 1973.

Workout alone by choice. In summer they are in their own pool and in winter they may swim at a local country club. They average between 1700 to 2000 yards per workout, 5 days a week.

Philosophy: both would prefer to have a coach for stroke feedback but it is not convenient to swim at a pool where there is coaching.

Cross training: Edie does weight training on a regular basis while Dan occasionally works out with weights, but Dan does use stretch cords for flexibility.

Jordan (66) and Marian Wolle (66)

This couple live in New Mexico but swim for Arizona Masters. Work out with a kid's team at New Mexico State University which is the only convenient year round pool. Workouts are coached but geared toward the younger swimmer. They swim 5 days a week, about 3000 yards per workout.

Philosophy: Marian started Masters swimming as a result of her first husband's heart attack. She wanted to be physically fit. No previous competitive training.

Both wish they had a Masters team as they find it difficult to swim on the same interval as the youngsters. On the plus side, the energetic enthusiasm of the kids is good for them.

Cross training: Neither swimmer uses weight training.

BUCKEYE MASTERS, OHIO

Yoshi Oyakawa (60)

Coached senior high school swim teams in Ohio for 32 years. Has worked out with a team but is now working out alone by choice.

Philosophy: Workouts are based on mileage and Costilli research that advocates less yardage but high quality with each workout. Worked out with the Cincinnati Marlins for two and a half months but found the 5600 yard workouts left his body depleted of potassium, although his repeats were good.

After looking at research he has incorporated more kicking drills as a regular part of training, resulting in seconds off his 100 backstroke time.

Cross training: Uses weights occasionally along with some cycling.

COLONIAL 1776, DELAWARE VALLEY

Cost: $15.00 per year as the club pays for them to swim.

Jeanne Merryman (74)

Past AAU competitor in Senior events for 6 years. Held the backstroke championship, joined Masters program in 1974.

Workouts: Swims at upper main line Y pool in Pennsylvania where there are several 25 yard pools (some for Masters and others for lap swimming). Swims 5 days a weeks, about 2200 to 2500 yards per workout.

Coached workouts that are varied. In the fall, there are stroke drills, starts and turns, then endurance swimming. Swimmers range in age from 20 to 71 with several open water swimmers and triathletes who want endurance training.

Philosophy: Loves to swim and compete. She also competes to eat and can eat more when competing. A social group that gets together after workout to eat, have parties, picnics.

Cross training: There are weight rooms at the Y with a swim bench. Stretching is encouraged before and after swims.

GOLD COAST MASTERS, FLORIDA

Workouts offered at different pools. Fort Lauderdale has 5 coached AM and PM workouts per week plus a Saturday workout.

June Krauser (72)

A past AAU competitor in high school and at Purdue, instrumental role in the inception of US Master program and its continued success.

Workouts: Swims at Fort Lauderdale pool, 5 to 6 times per week, around 3000 yards per workout. Does her own individualized workout by choice; there is a coached workout available.

Philosophy: Did not have a coach until 1986. Many coaches have come and gone since then. June lets the new coach know what she needs to stay in shape and then plans her own sets and intervals.

Cross training: There are weights at the pool. Workouts 1/2 hour 3 times a week. Plays golf. No stretching exercises.

Anne McGuire (63)

Past AAU competitor in high school and at Purdue. Started Masters program in 1973

Workouts: Coached workouts are offered but coach does not interact with swimmers. Swims 3000–3500 yards 5 times a week. Usually has a lane by herself and works out alone. Coach gives taper workouts.

Philosophy: Would like input from a coach, would prefer to work out with swimmer of same ability. Loves to compete; would never give up swimming at meets.

Cross Training: Runs 5 miles 4 times a week, plays golf every day. Teaches a water fitness class (involves stretching), does not do additional weights.

HOLMES JAX, FLORIDA

Florence Carr (72)

Flo is a Masters swimmer and a coach of Sun City Retirement Center. She is a past synchro performer who turned competitor as an adult. She swam for Rinconada Masters, CA, until her move to Florida in late 1980's. Her profile is under the coaches section.

Roger Holmes (75)

Founder and owner of the Holmes Lumberjacks in Florida. Roger is a past competitor for the University of Florida.

Workout: Three workouts a week, same for all ages. Roger may workout alone during the week as it is more convenient. He works out with the team on Saturday and coach allows him to do his own quality workout. Coach is young and still competes himself.

Cross training: Roger uses a swim bench in addition to workouts.

JERSEY MASTERS, NEW JERSEY

Many individual teams but at national meets they compete as a state team.

Ellie Trevison (54)

Never swam before Masters, was encouraged by her husband to swim.

Works out alone at the YWHA where swims 3 to 4 times a week, averaging 1500 yards per workout. Her husband organizes the workouts. Uses *Swim Magazine* and friends for workout ideas. Uses a pace clock.

Philosophy: Enjoys Masters swimming for fitness and social environment.

Cross training: None.

Jerry Markoff (66)

A past competitor in high school and college, started Masters swimming in 1980.

Works out on his own as there are limited facilities. Uses magazines for workout ideas. Swims 4 times a week, about 2000 yards per workout.

Philosophy: "How well you do it is not as important as doing it."

Cross training: Uses weights about once a week.

LAKESIDE MASTERS, KENTUCKY

Maryann Stone (60)

A noncompetitor prior to Masters.

Workout: Coached with beginner, fitness and competitive levels. One level has 1500 –2000 yards while other level is 3000–3500 yards.

Workouts are hard but can do them if she pushes. Some older swimmers need more rest and shorter yardage. Coach is middle age and a past competitor. Workouts are varied and stroke work is part of the regular workout.

Philosophy: Swims because she wants to feel good after the workout!

Cross training: None.

Ted Wathen (47)

A past competitor in high school and college, joined Masters in 1987 due to a friend's encouragement.

Workout: Coached. Swims 3 times a week, about 2300 –2500 meters each workout.

Philosophy: Ted had vowed never to swim again but likes Masters for health and endorphins. Wants and likes an organized workout.

Cross training: Includes running from fall to May and cycling twice a week.

LINCOLN MASTERS, ILLINOIS

This is a state team made up of many individual teams. At national meets they swim as one team. Local meets have individual teams competing.

Betty Bennett (54)

Past competitor in high school. Joined Masters in 1975 and swims for Palatine team which placed second in the state meet.

Workout: Coached and varied, mostly interval training. Most swimmers are young, competitive and there are a few lap swimmers or triathletes. Lanes offer different speeds. Works out 3 times a week, 10,000 yards per week. Coach is young and competes.

Philosophy: Important to put in 10,000 yards per week. Swims for health, which has prevented back surgery. Also needs companionship of other swimmers. Uses fins for shoulder problem.

Cross training: Uses weight training for arms one day and then legs the next day.

Irene David (53)

A competitor in high school, started Masters when she was 28.

Workout: Coached, individual workouts are according to lanes but geared more toward triathletes. Not enough people in her category to justify changing the workout to sprints rather than distance.

Works out 3 to 4 times a week, averaging between 2500 –3000 yards.

Philosophy: Would like more stroke work and individual tapering for big meets.

Cross training: Uses weights twice a week.

LOS ALTOS MASTERS, CALIFORNIA

Cost: $40.00 per month with cheaper rate for yearly dues and Senior citizens. Operated by a Board of Directors. Pool is outdoors with 7 lanes. Morning, noon and evening coached workouts offered every day.

Carolyn Boak (53)

Past competitor from age 13 –18 at Arden Hills Country Club, Sacramento. Joined Masters in 1977.

Workouts: Coached, lanes grouped according to ability. Swims 3 to 5 times a week, 3500–4000 yards in 1 hour and 15 minutes.

Philosophy: People over age 50 need a longer warm-up, especially before sprints. Need to be more gentle with stretching and to rest more as recovery rate is longer with aging. Sprint training is harder on the body than longer distances; therefore, must train at least once a week in order to do sprint well and reduce chance of injury. Most coaches and swimmers are too hung up on yardage. Swimmers feel they will get out of shape with longer rest and more taper. Keeps swimming for the "endorphin effect". Workout gives her a sense of accomplishment.

Cross training: Weights twice a week plus stretching.

Dave Gray (48)

Past competitor in high school and college, joined Masters in 1977. Is both a coach and a Masters competitor.

Workouts: Coached, lanes are grouped by ability and workouts are challenging with enough rest. Eight lane pool with one lane for lap swimmers. Works out 4 to 7 times a week; yardage is between 4000–5500 yards each workout.

Cross training: Planning to add weight training.

Della Sehorn (70)

A past competitor, swam in the 1952 Olympics. Her husband was her coach. Works out 4 days a week, 3000 to 3500 yards each workout.

Workouts: Coached. Includes triathletes and lap swimmers. All do the same workout but yardage and intervals vary according to lanes.

Philosophy: Swims for social interaction and fitness. Being the oldest swimmer on the team, she would like longer intervals between sets and more stroke correction, using video for corrections. Need increased tapering instruction.

Cross training: None.

Jim Triolo (84)

A past competitor in high school and college, swam for the Athens Club in Oakland until 1936 and joined Master team in 1993.

Workouts: Swim straight yardage by choice with some direction from a coach, prefers long distance events. Does not do kick drills or work with fins, paddles.

Philosophy: Swam only open water swims from 1968 until 1993. Still swims open water events but also competes at local and national meets.

Cross Training: Walks 2 miles on alternate swim days, plays golf.

MOVY, WICHITA, KANSAS

Betty Christian (75)

Past swimmer and diver in high school and college, joined Masters swimming and diving in 1980 after a 40 year layoff.

Workouts: Coached, only for Masters but includes a lot of triathletes. About 15—18 people in varied workouts. Coach understands the older swimmer and fits the workout to the person, may ask, "How far do you feel like going today?" Swims 3 times a week for 1200–1400 yards. Dives twice a week.

Philosophy: Enjoys the other people involved in swimming.

Cross training: None.

NEW ENGLAND MASTERS

Carol Adams (53)

Competed between 8 and 14 years of age, joined Masters team in January of 1994, hired a stroke coach for the FINA competition.

Workout: Coached with the YMCA Masters. Only one hour available for workout.

Philosophy: Frustrated by the number of people in one lane. Would like to see more times to swim. Great attitude, "Masters swimming makes getting older, younger." Also, "Where outside of swimming do people want to get older?"

Pat Pettersen (62)

Past competitor.

Workout: Alone since hour and location of pool is not convenient. She is free from 1PM to 2 PM in the afternoon and 6 AM workout is not appealing. Likes a lane to herself; finds it distracting to workout with others. Swims 3 times a week, about 600–700 yards a workout.

Cross training: Uses stretch cords and occasionally 3 pound weights.

Jim Edwards (74)

Past high school and college competitor.

Workouts: Works out alone at Brown University as times are not convenient with the team workout schedules. Designs his own workouts. Swims 6 times a week, averaging 2500 to 3000 yards per workout. Does not do enough interval workouts.

Cross training: Used stretch cords for the last four months, does not use weights.

MICHIGAN MASTERS

Composed of several teams that compete as a state team at national events. At local events, individual teams compete against one another. Good facilities for pools.

Dennis Me Manus (49)

No previous competitive training.

Workouts: Coached, ages from 28—65 with three workouts offered (slow, medium, fast). About 60 to 70 members who are scattered at various pools. Swims for South Oakland

Seals, won championships for last 6 years. Workouts are varied with both sprints and distance. Have access to 25 yard and 50 meter pools. But Tuesday and Thursday only in winter and Monday, Tuesday, Thursday in summer. His coach is a past competitor.

Cross training: None.

MULTNOMAH ATHLETIC CLUB, OREGON

Cost: Part of membership in a sports club.

Lavelle Stoinoff (61)

Past competitor from age 13 – 19, swam with a kids group at the club until a Masters program evolved. Joined Masters swimming at age 44.

Workout: Coached. Multnomah is a large club for all sports, therefore the coach directs all water oriented activities. Swims 6 days a week; yardage is about 5000 yards per workout.

Philosophy: Important to learn to swim as a child because development for swimming is accelerated; a disadvantage to learn later in life. Buoyancy and body position are very important. Pool temperature is important for the older swimmer—does not adjust to changes. Important for a coach to listen to the older swimmer, especially when they need more rest. No two people alike. The older swimmer requires special guidelines on how to taper and warm-up.

Cross training: Started running at age 40 about 3 to 5 miles, 4 times a week. Weights every 3 days for 40 minutes, uses tubing every other day.

O*H* I*O*, OHIO

George Rafter (80)

Swam in high school and for YMCA.

Workouts: No coach. Reads magazines and articles for workout ideas. Swims 5 days a week, about 2200 yards per workout, has access to 50 meter pool.

Philosophy: Works out alone as swimmers on the team are too fast and triathletes are too slow; doesn't understand swim terminology.

Dexter Woodford (83)

Past competitor in high school, YMCA, and Ohio State

Workout: Works out alone as distance across town to a team pool is too far. Does both sprints and distance, swims 5 days a week at YMCA, about 1 to 1 1/2 miles.

Philosophy: Important to get his heart rate up.

Cross training: You add up the miles! Also walks 2 miles, 5 times a week. Celebrated 80th birthday in the following manner: walked 4.5 miles to the pool at 7:00 AM, swam 4 miles, walked 3 miles to lunch, walked 3 miles back to YMCA pool, swam 2 miles at pool, walked 4.5 miles back home at 5:45 PM. Whew! Oh, and went to important Sierra Club meeting.

OJAI VALLEY MASTERS, SANTA BARBARA, CALIFORNIA

Grace Altus (73)

Workout: Coached— two choices of workouts each day. Have few competitors on team, mostly young triathletes. Lanes are divided according to abilities; sprints are part of the workout. Swims 5 days a week, about 2500 yards per workout.

Philosophy: Would like more people who went to meets. Stroke work is limited. There is a lot of freestyle.

Cross training: None.

Malchia Olshan (66)

Joined the Masters program in 1978 with no previous experience.

Workout: Coached with varied workouts both sprint and distance. Four workout choices: animals, technique class, less yardage, animals. Older swimmer may wear flippers and cut yardage. Swims for 1 hour, 3 times a week in the harder workout.

Philosophy: Swims for flexibility, and release of endorphins.

Cross training: Yoga class twice a week but does 1/2 hour of yoga each morning. Walks 2 to 3 miles several times a week.

OKMS, OKLAHOMA

Suzanne Robbins (63)

Joined 20 years ago.

Workouts: Works out alone as college team pool is too far away. Designs own workout (warm-up, intervals, mostly backstroke). Swims 5 days a week, about 1 mile each time.

Philosophy: Swims for mental and physical health. Misses the stroke critique that she received when coached.

Cross training: No weight training.

RINCONADA MASTERS, CALIFORNIA

Cost: $30.00 per month with optional $5.00 surcharge for Saturday and Sunday swims.

Pool: Outdoor pool with 14 lanes. Eight coached workouts times offered Monday through Friday with one assistant-coached workout on Saturday and Sunday.

Dick Bennett (66)

Past competitor in high school and college but never a medalist. Started with Masters program in 1977.

Workouts: Coached swims. Lack proper sprint workouts. Most workout intervals are short. Sprinters need long rest with a fast swim! Don't work enough on starts and turns - should be practiced throughout the season, not just at competition time.

Philosophy: Important to write down goals for the season and then form a workout plan with the coach toward those goals. Example, in 1996, Dick planned to do the 200 free in 2:06. Swims because he likes competition — was not able to win medals in his youth so he now enjoys winning events at Nationals. Also, his body likes to have exercise.

Cross training: In the past have run and swum on alternate days.

Aldo Da Rosa (80)

Past competitor (high school) in Brazil in running. Also swam free and backstroke at private sports club in Brazil. Continued to train in running at Stanford until he broke his leg, switched to lap swimming for exercise. Joined Masters team in 1976 when friend talked him into swimming on a relay for Rinconada, won a national record and was hooked!

Workouts: Coached. Used to swim 7 days a week; now finds that he swims better with a couple of days of rest. Yardage is 3000 to 3500 yards per workout.

Philosophy: Important to have structured workout but also some unstructured time that includes more breaststroke drills and kicks. Gets withdrawal symptoms if he does not swim. Keeps a daily record of yardage, weight, amount of sleep, naps, blood pressure.

Cross training: Flexibility exercises every day that include 20 sit-ups, 12 chin-ups, timed stand on one foot for balance, deep knee bends and stationary bike. Also Cybex weights at YMCA 3 times a week.

Jack Halliday (61)

Past competitor in college. Joined Rinconada Masters in 1981 after 23 year layoff.

Workouts: Coached. Swims 4 to 6 times a week, about 2500–3500 meters. Works out in long course pool all year.

Philosophy: Older swimmers need longer warm-ups and warm-downs. Important to get stroke work in even when others do nothing but freestyle. Spends more time on stroke technique than yardage per se. Developing good techniques pays off in longer races.

Cross Training: None.

Ann Kay (63)

No previous competition prior to joining a Masters team at age 36.

Workouts: Quality workout is more important than yardage as one ages. Also need to have more rest and then swim fast. If you practice slow, then you will end up competing slow. Need a longer warm-up than younger swimmers.

Philosophy: Can't power through a race as one gets older; therefore, improved technique becomes very important in the aging process. Don't use younger kids workouts for older swimmers, as leg power declines in the aging process. Kick drills must be worked hard, not used as rest. Write down a specific set of goals for the season, include yardage, swim times in workouts and how the body feels each workout. Keep track of body weight and relate to swim time performance. Helps to change goals. Swims because of the other people talking, sharing ideas in the lanes and locker room.

Cross training: Low weights with fast repetitions 3 times a week.

Sue Kelly (50)

Past youth competitor for the Palo Alto Swim Club. Swim coach for kids and a Master competitor.

Workouts: Mostly coached workouts at Rinconada but may also swim alone in pool with her team. Swims 4 times a week, about 3000 yards per workout.

Philosophy: It is necessary to have all-round workout that includes endurance training as well as sprint training. Workouts are not geared toward the sprinter — so before competition she modifies the workout to shorter distances, longer intervals and faster swimming. Feels coaches in general do not offer sprint training as it requires more planning and work. Likes the discipline of working with other swimmers — keeps her working on all strokes. Also, where else can you rub elbows with beautiful male bodies.

Cross training: Has done aerobics in the past until an injury. Trained with weights to build up upper body for her job.

ROCKY MOUNTAIN MASTERS, COLORADO

Liz Stock (63)

No past competition. Started swimming at 48 years of age (coach talked her into a regional meet and she stayed swimming).

Workouts: At the YMCA that include a separate coached Masters and preMasters workout. There is a noon and evening workout for Masters but program includes a lot of triathletes. Swims 3 days a week, about 800 meters in the summer at 50 meter pool. Coach is young, went to Olympic trials.

Philosophy: Would like a program for older, slower people where she could improve. swims for health, to lose weight, would like to swim faster.

Cross training: Uses stationary bike and weights 3 times a week.

SACRAMENTO MASTERS, CALIFORNIA

Anita Hazen (69)

No past competition, joined Masters in 1992.

Workout: Works out 3 days a week with Dick Smith. The other 4 days by herself. Access to 25 yard and 50 meter pools. Minimum of 1650 yards but some days it is a lot more.

Philosophy: Must work out at least 1650 yards a day or "Nothing goes right for the rest of the day." Prefers long distances to sprints. Swimming faster this year, attributes it to regular workouts with Dick 3 times a week rather than just swimming by herself.

Cross training: None.

Dick Smith (74)

Workout: Works out alone by choice at Arden Hills Country Club pool. Team pools are scattered and inconvenient, some just for kids. Access to 25 yard and 50 meter pools. Swims every day for 2500 yards.

Cross training: Uses a Nordic track every other day, no weight training.

SAN DIEGO SWIM MASTERS

Workouts offered at different pools. 5 workouts per day are offered at UC San Diego.

Jim Jones (70)

High school and collegiate swimmer (one of top 6 freestyle swimmers in the world in 1950 –51), joined Masters 1995.

Workouts: Travels a lot, workouts are wherever he can find a pool, usually at YMCA. Works out alone.

Philosophy: Out of swimming for 41 years. Had cardiovascular surgery and came back to swimming for health reasons. Says it feels good to be back competing.

Cross Training: No weights, no stretching

Betsy Jordan (61)

Past AAU swimmer until age 19, joined Masters at age 34.

Workouts: Workouts are coached with tapers. Swims 2500–3000 yards 5 times a week with people of same ability in a lane.

Philosophy: Coach makes the difference in enjoyment of workouts. Our coach is great! Has the ability to tailor workout to needs of the individual. Works equally well with triathletes or swim competitors. Good motivator and makes the workout FUN.

Cross Training: Weights both free and machine for the past 6 years. Works out 3 times a week for 45 minute sessions. Offered through the swim club. No stretching.

Pete Riddle (60)

Joined Masters about 10 years ago. Husband of Betsy Jordan.

Workouts: Workouts are coached with tapers. Swims 2500–3000 yards 5 times a week with people of same ability in a lane.

Cross Training: Runs 2 times a week in addition to weights.

SAN MATEO MARLINS, CALIFORNIA

Helen Roumasset (82)

Started Masters program 19 years ago.

Workouts: Coach adjusts workouts for older swimmers. Swims in a 25 meter pool, 3 times a week, about 1300 meters each workout.

Philosophy: Swims for health (has asthma); also workouts makes her feel more alive! Would like to see more butterfly and back instruction using the breaststroke kick during workouts.

Cross training: None.

Ray (78) and Zada (77) Taft - see coach section for more detail

Ray was Olympic contender in 1940, games canceled due to war.

Both have been Master swimmers since 1969.

Workout: Coached, swim 3 to 4 times a week. Zada does 1200 -1500 meters each workout. Ray puts in 1800 meters per workout.

Philosophy: Swim for friendship, laughter, chance to travel to new places, keeps you physically fit.

STANFORD MASTERS, CALIFORNIA

Margery Sharpe (81)

Started a Master program in 1991, swam only open water events for two years.

Workouts: Coached. Swims in 50 meter and 25 yard pool, 2500–3000 yards, 3 times a week. Until this year she has concentrated on 2 miles open water swims and the 1650 free. Coach trained her to swim all freestyle distances this year for the Nationals in Washington and Orlando.

Philosophy: Has had 3 operations on her back and swims for health, flexibility and has amazed her doctor. Enjoys the other swimmers, likes the social aspect of a team.

TAMALPAIS MASTERS, CALIFORNIA

Nancy Rideout (55)

Past competitor, joined Masters in 1972.

Workout: Coached. Have an older team (many swimmers are over 45), not a lot of competitive swimmers. Workouts are varied but geared toward the fastest swimmer, but each lane sets its own intervals. Her lane even tapered with her for FINA meet. Swims all strokes.

Cross training: None. Performs a stretch routine twice a day.

Charlotte Jenkins (58)

Joined Masters program in 1975.

Workout: Coached. Workouts are 6 days a week, 5 narrow lanes in a 25 yard outdoor pool. Swims 5 days a week, about 3000 yards per workout. Each lane has a spokesperson who adjusts the workout according to the ability of the swimmers. This is okay with the coach. Maintain their own pool; must do fund-raising. Cost is $45.00 month.

Philosophy: Team is composed of more swimmers in the 45–50 age group with few competitors. Would like to see more swimmers interested in going to meets.

Cross training: Started cycling.

Dore Schwab (74)

Joined Masters when he was 50 years of age.

Workout: Coached. Works out 4 to 5 times a week, uses Zoomers on kicking set.

Philosophy: Observed a decline in swim performance about age 66 — could no longer sprint as fast. Not as serious about competing as he has aged. Enjoys the social aspects of swimming with a team. Is involved with the organization of Pacific Masters Association.

THE OLYMPIC CLUB, SAN FRANCISCO, CALIFORNIA

Margery Meyer (75)

Joined Masters 11 years ago at age 64 with no previous competition training.

Workout: Coached for the last 3 years, part of a small swim class at Monterey Peninsula College which includes a lot of individual attention. Previous years were without a coach. Swims minimum of 4 times a week, approximately 2400–3600 yards per workout. Coach knows how to train and is always on deck to record times. Gives plenty of rest. Taper workouts well done. Feels prepared for meets.

A typical workout (after a warm-up): repeat 6 times with all out swims 100 yards on the 3 minutes, 50 yards on the 2 minutes, and 25 yards on the minute.

Philosophy: She calls herself a born competitor, "likes to win." Attributes improved times to her "seasoned" coach who is geared toward competition and knows her potential times. He is realistic but not afraid to push her. She is more focused and motivated now than when she first started Masters swimming.

Cross Training: Does some weight training but not a lot.

VIRGINIA MASTERS, VIRGINIA

Cost: Members $48.00 – $50.00 per month. Nonmembers $43.00 per month.

Chuck Wilmore (62)

Started swimming at 38; has been trying to catch up ever since. Has been serious about swimming for the last 16 years.

Workouts: Uses a community pool, swims alone as a lap swimmer. No coach as other clubs are about 100 miles away. Swims 3 to 4 times a week averaging 2000 to 3000 yards each time. Feels he has lousy workouts. Had been a triathlete in the past until a knee injury.

Philosophy: Not sure why he swims except that other swimmers are the nicest people in the world.

Cross training: None.

WALNUT CREEK MASTERS, CALIFORNIA

Cost: Yearly fee to the city for water usage. Monthly fee is $35.00. Yearly Senior citizen discount or $25.00 per month

Pool: 25 yard and 50 meter outdoor pool with adjacent weight room. Under the Recreation Department.

Don Brown (64)

Competed in high school, joined Masters program 21 years ago. Swims 3 to 4 times a week, about 2700 meters.

Workout: Coached. Two coaches for 260 swimmers, 25 yard and 50 meter pool. All ages but lanes are divided according to abilities. Swim where you feel comfortable, can move up or down a lane according to how you feel that day. Long course workouts are always creative but in a subtle way, start swimmers at both ends of the pool. Coach is always on deck and speaks to everyone.

Philosophy: Swim with peer group and for a social circle. Swims because people tend to repeat things they are good at. Thinks he has the greatest coach due to a positive attitude in the workout for all swimmers. No one on the team is slow, everyone is encouraged.

Cross training: Plays tennis.

Joan Alexander (65) and Donna Monroe (63)

Workouts: Coached. Two coaches. One gives hard workouts, the other coach gives easier workouts but is enthusiastic. Always glad to see swimmers. Workouts vary, Monday and Tuesday are hard (increased yardage), back off a little on Wednesday (more sprint work), Friday is hard. Both swim 4 to 5 days a week; yardage between 3000 – 3500 yards per workout.

10:30 AM workout for Seniors (pregnant women join this group but more are staying permanently).

Philosophy: Joan — "Don't assume I know anything"—would like more stroke technique. Donna ——swims with team because when swimming with someone else I push harder. Both swim for social contacts and fitness.

Cross Training: Joan walking and jogging, weights and bands. Donna takes a body conditioning class that includes weights, aerobics.

Jean Durston (84)

Joined the Masters 15 years ago.

Workouts: Swims 5 times a week, about a 2500 yard workout. Follows the same coached workout as everyone else. Her warm-down may include a slow 400 IM.

Philosophy: Likes to feel good, swims for health and companionship. Has many older swimmer friends on the team.

Cross Training: Performs stretching exercise in bed before getting up and throughout the day while at home.

Jae Howell (74)

Swim school for 35 years, synchronized swimming and swim lessons. Synchro team was 2nd nationally and in world competition.

Workout: Coached but also works out alone as she knows what to emphasize. Workouts are varied. Several choices throughout the day, both 25 yard and 50 meter distances, yardage adjusted for age differences.

Philosophy: Would like to see more butterfly, breaststroke drills and more critique on strokes. Swims 5 to 6 times a week, about 2400 yards each workout.

Cross training: Uses 3 pound weights on arms at home during commercials. Plays tennis.

INDIVIDUAL COACH'S PROFILES.

Coaches are listed alphabetically.

Cindy Baxter (65)   Rinconada Masters, Palo Alto, CA

Coach and Masters competitor, Cindy has been coaching Masters program with Carol Macpherson for 25 years. Also has taught private and recreation preschool swim program for 28 years.

Workouts: Offers 4 different workouts Monday through Friday in a 16 lane, 25 yard, outdoor pool. Each workout has different yardage, ranging from 2000 yards to 4000 yards with different interval times. Older swimmers can find a lane compatible with ability. Ages are mixed in the lanes according to ability. One assistant-coached workout is available on Saturday and Sunday. Wednesdays are fin days, more yardage.

Fall emphasizes long-distance training (more 500, 800, 1000 sets). Spring is more short distances (50, 100's). Advise weight training with caution and stretch cords are encouraged. Under auspices of the Palo Alto Recreation Department.

Philosophy: Very important to have goals. Noncompetitor may have a goal of being able to finish the workout or learn to do the butterfly.   Competitors are more goal-oriented with a high energy level. It is good to mix these two groups in the lanes as the noncompetitors will pick up the energy level. It is important to emphasize teaching techniques to new swimmers and as they get excited and improve, then concentrate on coaching. Also, important to be enthusiastic and share the excitement with the swimmer as he excels in a new area. Age is not as important as ability level in a lane. Older swimmers are a role model for younger swimmers.

Cost: $30.00 per month with additional $5.00 for those who wish to swim weekends.

Florence Carr (72) - Sun City Center, FL

Coaches at a retirement village near Tampa, Florida. Past synchronized competitor also competes for Holmes JAX Masters.

Workouts: Offers 4 workouts a week for 1 and 1/2 hours each time. One workout for everyone; gets ideas from Marianne Brems' book on *100 workouts*.

Philosophy: Most of her swimmers never swam before and are over 55. They need to learn interval training, working with a pace clock. Always want to know "WHY". These people are not typical Master swimmers; get upset if their pulse goes over 150.

Cost: Unknown.

Wanda Cavanaugh (57) Rinconada Masters, CA

Past competitor, swam in Pan American Games in 1955. A past age-group coach for several different teams and past coach for De Anza Masters. She now competes in Masters, mostly open water swims.

Philosophy: Older swimmers are better at following some directions such as drills but not good at following complicated workouts that require a lot of changes. Older swimmers may swim as fast as younger swimmer but their recovery rate is slower so the workout needs to be adjusted to fit their needs. Emphasized an IM basis for workouts to develop all strokes.

Michael Collins (31) Davis Aquatic Masters, CA

Competed in high school and college. Started coaching at 16 with a summer recreation team. In 1987, started coaching a Masters team. In 1989, became Davis coach. Also competes as a Master swimmer.

Workouts: 8 lane outdoor pool with 8 one hour workouts offered each day. One workout each day is for Seniors. They get double the rest (at least 20 seconds). Work on speed and turnover rate. Nonprofit organization with 360 swimmers. No space or time to do dry land exercises.

Philosophy: Older swimmers usually have good endurance but turnover rate decreases. Use fins 1 to 2 times a week to get them to feel moving faster and how to go forward. Work on technique, as flexibility decreases, elbows drop. Encourage them to do new strokes and be honest about expectations as one ages. Be a realistic coach. Therefore, do not expect perfection but challenge their limits.

Cost: $25.00 for Senior citizens, $30.00 per month for regulars. Swimmers over 80 are free, to encourage the older person to swim.

Rick Goeden (50)   Ojai Valley Racquet Club, CA

Started coaching in 1972 to age-groupers in Wisconsin. Now coaches mostly Masters but still offers kid swim lessons.

Workouts: Outdoor pool that offers workouts 5 days a week with 4 different workoutsbeing geared to different levels of swimming. Three of the harder workouts have fewer older swimmers but those who come can put on flippers if the interval is too short. Rest interval is longer in the easier workouts.

Philosophy: Influenced by Doc Councilman. Advocates learning all strokes; workouts are varied to keep interest level high. Offers good private lessons with underwater video. Encourages swimmers to do weight training and stretching. There is a lot of positive team camaraderie and competitive spirit.

Dave Gray (51)   Los Altos Masters, Los Altos, CA

Coached age-group swimmers on part-time basis then coached at College of San Mateo for 2 years. Has filled in as a Master coach for a number of years at both San Mateo and Los Altos Master programs. Also competes as a Masters swimmer.

Workouts: 8 lane outdoor pool, meters at San Mateo and yards at Los Altos. Includes triathletes and lap swimmers — lot of young swimmers at Los Altos Masters. Workout offered every day — three times daily during the week and twice on weekends. Managed by a Board of Directors.

Philosophy: Feels that the older swimmer is more independent and the motivation for performance is different than for younger swimmers. Must understand this motivation.

Cost: Los Altos Masters $40.00 each month with a discount for yearly payment and Senior citizens.

Carol Macpherson (58)   Rinconada Masters, CA

Carol has been coaching with Cindy Baxter for 25 years, Masters program only, no lap swimmers. Taught swim lessons for 28 years. Swam competitively for George Haines at Santa Clara Swim Club. Also competes as a Master swimmer.

Workouts: Offers 4 different workouts Monday through Friday in a 16 lane, 25 yard outdoor pool. Each workout has different yardage, ranging from 2000 to 4000 yards with different interval times. Older swimmers can find a lane compatible with ability. Ages are mixed in the lanes according to ability. One assistant-coached workout is available on Saturday and Sunday. Wednesdays are fin days, more yardage. Fall has long distance training (more 500, 800, 1000 sets), spring more shorter distances (50, 100's). Use of stretch cords and weight training are recommended with caution. Master program is under the auspices of the Palo Alto Recreation Department.

Philosophy: Swimmer techniques differ between under 50 and over 50 years of age. Most younger swimmers have previous training in racing instruction and psyching up for competition. The over 50 group requires additional training to get ready for a meet, including stroke visualization and tapering techniques. They need more encouragement than younger swimmers. Therefore, coaches must adapt their instructions as swimmers age. Weight training helps the older swimmer gain muscle strength while stretch cords encourage flexibility.

Cost: $30.00 per month with extra $5.00 for those who wish to swim weekends.

Jim Miller (47) Virginia Masters, VA

Past competitor. Started coaching in 1981 and became involved with the Masters as an extension of working with the older athlete (profession is a physician).

Workouts: Offers 14 practices per week with distances that range from 1500 to 4000 yards depending on lane and ability. Workouts last one hour to one and one quarter hour. Emphasis on stroke technique and a good aerobic base for the individual athlete.

Philosophy: Feels the water is a good medium for older individuals to continue performing at a high level without injuries to the body. Teach younger and older swimmers the same, just recalibrate time intervals. Exception would be for individuals who develop physical disabilities. Then it may be necessary to teach different types of open turns or substitute the breast stroke kick for the dolphin in butterfly. Have learned a lot from older swimmers — seen a tremendous improvement in times that was not expected. Encourages the use of stretch cords and weights; offers a clinic in this areas with the help of an exercise physiologist. To keep up club enthusiasm, active group participation in side trips to volleyball and softball games are offered for competitive and fitness swimmers.

Cost: Members $48.00–$50.00 per month. Nonmembers $43.00 per month.

Kerry O'Brien (40) Walnut Creek Masters, CA

Age group competitor. Has been coaching 22 years with 17 years as a Masters coach. Also competes as a Masters swimmer.

Workouts: Offers 18 workouts per week in a 50 meter or 25 yard, outdoor pool. Lanes are arranged according to ability. Workout offered at 10:30 AM for older swimmers where yardage and rest is adjusted. Weight training offered in the facility, heavy during short course. Surgical tubing 3 times a week, 1/2 hour before workout.

Philosophy: Must be tuned into the body, take heart rate. Listen to the older swimmer but don't coddle them; they are as serious as the younger swimmer so treat them the same but be flexible with workouts. Keep swimmer happy; they need to feel good about pace in the water. Be enthusiastic. Tapering for the older swimmer needs to be started sooner than for the younger swimmer.

Cost: Yearly fee to the city for water usage. Monthly fee is $35.00 with a Senior citizen discount at $25.00.

Gail Roper (68) USF Masters, San Francisco, CA

Swam in the 1952 Olympics, National AAU swimmer and 200 titles. Coaches and competes as a Master swimmer.

Workouts: 8 lane, 25 yard, indoor pool, part of the University of San Francisco facilities. Offers 10 workouts per week; workout in lanes will change each day depending on who shows up. Lanes may specialize, i.e. IM lane and a backstroke lane. May have 4 different workouts going at the same time. Always provide stroke work for motivation. Weight training is offered at the facility and included in the cost per month.

Philosophy: Goals are clear, training for short course championships in April. All swimmers are expected to participate. Triathletes are not accepted into program if they won't comply with goals. Primary goal is to give them a good workout. Older swimmers are more difficult to coach than younger swimmers. Age-group swimmers are used to obeying and don't analyze what you tell them. Older swimmers have different agendas with a mixture of triathletes, competitors and noncompetitors.

Cost: $54.00 month includes swim workouts, weights, locker room facilities.

Ray (75) and Zada Taft (74) San Mateo Marlins, San Mateo, CA

Ray made the Olympic team in 1940 but war canceled the event. Also excelled in boxing. Coached and taught swimming for 31 years, both compete and hold many records in the Masters program. Ray started teaching swimming in 1953 at The Olympic Club in San Francisco. Ray and Zada had a swim school in Burlingame, CA, where they taught all age levels.

Workouts: Started San Mateo Marlins in 1969, coached in an 8 lane, 25 meter outdoor pool where each lane is geared to the peer level of that lane. Retired in 1990. Under auspices of the San Mateo Recreation Department.

Philosophy: Pool is always 81 degrees which is important to many older swimmers. Swimmers receive individual help if they ask. Important to keep the program fun but very low key. Zada always corrects strokes; feels it is important to have correct stroke mechanics. Master coaching is easier than age group because discipline is not necessary.

Cost: Separate programs for lap and Master programs. $40.00 monthly or $102.00 quarterly with a discount for Senior citizens.

Bill Tingley (46) Lakeside Masters, Louisville, KT

Bill was All American swimmer at Southern Illinois University. Has coached a Masters team only for the past 18 years.

Workouts: Offers one workout but the yardage is varied into 2 levels. One level is at 1500 to 2000 yards while the second levels provides 3000 to 3500 yards. Stroke work is offered at both levels.

Philosophy: With the older swimmer, "You have to understand their lifestyle and what is important to them." Some people want a personal trainer which is not possible with a large team. Must be flexible as a coach.

SWIMMERS OUTSIDE THE UNITED STATES.

Swimmers are listed under the country they represent. The countries are listed alphabetically.

AUSTRALIA

Brian Luxton (67) competitor

Swims for Toowoomba, Queensland, which is second largest club in Australia. High school competitor. Master swimmer for 13 years.

Workouts: Coached workouts. The coach's job is voluntary, therefore coaches do not remain for a long time and move on to a paid position. Present coach also has a young children's team, adjusts to working with adults very well, flexible. Workouts for adults are varied and lanes are adjusted according to ability.

Facilities: Has access to a 50 meter pool in the summer and a 25 yard pool in the winter. Does not do weight training although it is available.

Norma O'Brian (59) competitor and coach

Swims for Guilford (near Sydney). Has been a coach for 27 years.

Workouts: Aerobics is offered for swimmers on Sunday. Mostly distance workouts. Very social program with some interval training. Need a proper program for the older swimmer.

Facilities: Access to a 25 yard pool with 3e lanes, twice a week. Has access to other pools in the area, both 50 meter and 25 yard.

BRAZIL

Morel Bueno (54) competitor

Swims for Allsport in Curitiba. Started swimming with Masters at age 39.

Workouts: Has coached workouts 6 times a week. May swim twice a day, 1 hour each time, about 3500 meters total for the day. Does cross training, some weights and cycling. His main sport is volleyball.

Maria Lenk (82) competitor

Swims for Rio Masters. Competed in the 1932 Olympics at Los Angeles and again in 1936 in Berlin.

Workouts: She works out alone by choice. Physical Education was her career, so she relies on her knowledge plus Swim Magazine for workouts. A coach is useful but she uses the advice of a Russian coach who said "listen to your body." Her workouts are every day, around 2000–3000 meters if she swims fast, then the yardage is cut back.

Jose Carlos Pellegrino (66) competitor

Competed when young, then turned to water polo, tennis and soccer. Came back to swimming after he broke his feet and had a heart attack in 1987.

Workouts: Swims 4 to 6 times a week, about 2000 meters. No weight training but does stretching and flexibility exercises.

CANADA

Linda Brett (47) competitor. Toronto

Learned to swim at age 35. Joined Master team at age 40.

Workouts: Coached. Swims 3 times a week for a total of 9000 yards per week in the Jewish Community Center all year round. There are 4 workouts offered per week to all ages. Workouts offer stroke instruction, drills, intervals and are individualized for the swimmer.

Philosophy: Has been a competitor all her life and swimming offers competition and fitness. Oldest swimmer on the 15 member team. Group activities such as dinners and parties are offered for social activities.

Cross training: Aerobic classes each week plus weight training twice a week.

Kay Easun (66) competitor

Swims for North York of Metropolitan in Toronto. Swam with Masters team from 1977 to 1987; took a break and returned to competition this past year.

Philosophy: Fitness, participation and competition in that order when the swimmer is ready. She does not want to see time standards initiated for Master swimmers as it would limit the joy of competition for the slower swimmer. As a former coach, Kay feels that coaches must be flexible and willing to accept an older swimmer's limits. She encourages goal setting and invites swimmers to make a diary so that progress can be observed.

Thelma Roach (69) Canada ATB (Teddy Bears) competitor

Past competitor for 20 years.

Workouts: Swims 3 times a week about 2000–3000 yards per workout. All ages workout together— 25 to 75 years. Her husband coaches the team.

Philosophy: Swims to keep in condition. Enjoys the companionship of other swimmers. Team has a newsletter and parties.

Cross training: Bike riding and walking.

Dues: $195 per year to swim 3 times a week.

Ted Roach (72) Coach of Teddy Bears and competitor

Has coached Masters team for the past 23 years. Prior to that he coached age groupers and American Red Cross. Coaches because he enjoys it.

Philosophy: Masters program is very different from age groupers; need a longer warm-up. Can't give the same workout to kids and older adults. Do not recommend weights, hand paddles or stretch cords for swimmers over 40 years of age as it is not good for shoulders. It is best to swim without aids for maximum workout.

FRANCE

Monique Berlioux (73) competitor

Swims for Racing Club de France which is a private club.

Workouts: Adults are not encouraged to train, prevailing theory is that after ages 18 to 20 you are too old to swim. Coached workouts are for youngsters. No coach for older swimmers. Swims twice a week about 1500 kilometers — mostly backstroke.

Facilities: Pools are not readily available to adults — must use a private club that is not adapted to workouts. No weight training.

GERMANY

Grete Harnish (83) swims for SG Mainz, Lilo Hoschke (75), Gisela Petri (59) swims for SG Mainz

Workouts: These ladies workout at a family-type of private swim club that offers a 1 hour coached workout 4 times a week. Workouts are varied. Adults are encouraged to swim and train. Plenty of pool space. Swim mostly for fun and social gatherings.

Christel Vigener (56) - competitor

Swims for Steinhagen Amshausen.

Workouts: Coached. Offered for all ages. Mixture of distance and interval training with adjustments for the different ages. Swims 4 to 5 times a week, about 2000 meters. Does weight training and cycling.

GREAT BRITAIN

Jane Asher (66) competitor and coach, Norwich

Swam in a low key high school program during World War II in South Africa. Real interest and sport was horseback riding and jumping. Her father fostered a desire to succeed at competition. Jane entered the coaching field through teaching both private lessons and at clubs. Eventually a group of parents became her first Masters group which was 24 years ago. In the early 1980's, after moving to England, she began to get herself fit in swimming and also started a Masters program.

Workouts: Masters have workouts during the week, not on Saturday, mostly through classes that Jane teaches. No real team in Norfolk but once a year they have a fun meet with individuals participating from 25 to 74 years of age. There are Master teams in Liverpool and London. Jane tries to swim about 4 times a week, in various pools, averaging 2500 meters.

Philosophy: As a coach she feels the older swimmer needs more rest between sets than younger swimmers. Older swimmers need a moderate pace where flexibility becomes more important than cardiovascular enhancement. She has a fun, positive and constructive approach to coaching and her own success at swimming.

Facilities: All pools are indoors. In Norwich there are two 25 meter school pools used by children where Masters are not welcome! Other pools that do accept Master swimmers either lack lane lines, are open for limited hours and open to other noncompetitive swimmers. Masters do a lot of one arm drills, no backstroke and fly kick underwater.

Flora Connolley (64) competitor

Lives in Scotland but competes for Great Britain.

Workouts: Swims alone at a physical fitness center twice a week for under an hour. All ages swim together—12 swimmers total. Husband was a coach, critiques her strokes. Fantastic swimmer for the small amount of yardage in training. No weight training but does Scottish dancing which is a fun way to stay in shape.

JAPAN

People team brought 45 competitors to Santa Clara International meet. Fifteen swimmers were over age 50 with the oldest at 68 years of age.

Masayo Azuma (63) competitor

Swam in the 1952 Olympics. Master swimmer with People Futano (outside of Tokyo).

Workouts: Coached. Swims 3 times a week, approximately 1500 meters. Concentrates on her specialty, breaststroke. Set a world record in 100M and 200M breast.

Facilities: Swims in a 25 meter, indoor pool.

Michiko Tokano (63) competitor

Master swimmer with TDFK for 13 years in Tokyo.

Workouts: No coach for regular workouts. Workouts are whatever you want to do. She used an outside coach for one week to get ready for FINA competition. Swims mostly for fitness, about 2000 meters per workout.

Facilities: Has access to both 25 and 50 meter pools.

ISRAEL

Edith Thein (79) competitor

Swims for Arad Masters. Past competitor in Czechoslovakia. Competed in Jewish Olympics last year.

Workouts: Works out 5 to 6 days a week in a 25 meter pool, about two kilometers each workout. Husband coaches her, mostly backstroke training. Limited interval training with a pace clock. Israel has had a Masters Association for the last 5 years. Many swimming clubs are for ages 6 to 18.

ITALY

Renata Marting (60) competitor

Started the Swimming Federation program in Italy thirteen years ago. Have 18 to 20 meets per year with a ceremony at the end of the year to award prizes (medals, cups). Swimmers must compete in 5 different swims throughout the year to qualify. Only two races are offered at each meet because of size (1000 swimmers attend each meet which are well publicized events).

Facilities: Renata swims at a private club 2 to 3 times a week, between 2000–3000 meters per workout. Does not do sprints, just distance. Works out alone; does her own workouts (son was Olympic swimmer). No weight training.

NEW ZEALAND

Ailsa Jordan (51) competitor and coach for Northland Masters

Workouts are 4 times a week, 1800 meters. Thursday night is a hard workout. Both distance and sprints offered plus different paces. For stroke work they use underwater video and an outside expert.

Facilities: Access to 1 indoor pool. Schools have outdoor pools but need covers for year-round swimming. No weight training.

SOUTH AFRICA

Gloria Williamson (58) competitor

Swims for Highveld Transvaal.

Workouts: She works out on her own by choice, and has a friend who provides the workouts. She swims 5 days a week, about two kilometers each workout. She swims for health and recreation.

Facilities: Outdoor 33 yard heated pool is used in the summer. In winter the pool is indoor.

SWITZERLAND

Uta Schneider (48) competitor

Swims for Bremgarten. Past competitor. Joined Masters 25 years ago.

Workouts: There are 1 hour coached workouts with 8 to 9 older swimmers. Could workout with younger kid's team but prefers to work out alone at a private swim club. Swims 6 to 7 times a week, between 3000–4000 meters. Swims for personal health to handle stress. Also likes to set goals and see how other people swim. Swimming is a social occasion. Uses a Stepmaster for cross training.

Facilities: Has access to both a 25 and 50 meter pool.

Glossary

Appendix B

Aerobic	Refers to training in which intake of oxygen equals use of oxygen in muscles.
Anaerobic	Refers to training in which muscle cells lack sufficient oxygen.
Catch	A portion of the arm stroke that positions the hand to grab water.
Drag	Resistance of the water against the body.
Drill	An exercise designed to improve one specific part of a stroke.
Endorphin	A neuropeptide released in the brain that acts as a painkiller.
Lactic Acid	A natural breakdown product of muscle metabolism produced during periods of insufficient oxygen to muscles.
Layout	A stretched out position common to synchronized moves and dive executions.
Medley	A swim event that uses all four strokes swum in the order of backstroke, breaststroke, butterfly and freestyle.
Pace	To swim each lap of an event in the same time.

Pace Clock	A large stopwatch on the pool deck for swimmers to see swim times. Clocks are digital or have minute and second hands.
Pike	A body position used in dives in which the body is bent at the hips but the legs are straight.
Pull	A type of training drill that uses arms only.
Scull	A rotation movement of the hands to propel the body.
Set	Name for a whole group of repeat swims.
Taper	The period before competition in which workouts are designed to give the swimmer more rest to tune the body.
Tuck	A body position used in dives in which the body is bent at the hips and the knees.

NORM MANOOGIAN'S WEIGHT TRAINING EXERCISES FOR SWIMMERS								
STROKE	SETS REPS	1	2	3	4	5	6	
BACK STROKE								
1. Press behind neck	4 x 10							
2. Incline press	4 x 10							
3. Upright rowing	4 x 10							
4. Pulldown behind neck	4 x 10							
5. Lateral arm raises	4 x 10							
6. Shoulder shrugs	4 x 10							
7. Dumbbell swings	4 x 10							
8. Hack squats	4 x 10							
9. Lower leg extensions	4 x 20							
10. Lower leg flexions	4 x 15							
11. Horizontal straight leg raisers	30 total							
CRAWL STROKE								
1. Bench press	4 x 10							
2. Standing press	4 x 10							
3. Upright rowing	4 x 10							
4. Bentover rowing	4 x 10							
5. Triceps (overhead arm extensions)	4 x 10							
6. Bardips	20 total							
7. Supine bentarm pullovers	4 x 10							
8. Stiffleg deadlift	3 x 10							
9. Hack squats	4 x 10							
10. Horizontal straight leg raisers	30 total							
BREAST STROKE								
1. Bench press	4 x 10							
2. Power cleans	4 x 5							
3. Upright rowing	4 x 10							
4. Pulldown behind neck	4 x 10							
5. Triceps (overhead arm extensions)	4 x 10							
6. Bentarm pullovers	4 x 10							
7. Dumbbell swings	4 x 10							
8. Back hyperextensions	20 total							
9. Hack squats	4 x 10							
10. Lower leg extensions	4 x 20							
11. Lower leg flexions	4 x 15							
12. Horizontal straight leg raisers	30 total							
BUTTERFLY								
1. Bench press	4 x 10							
2. Press behind neck	4 x 10							
3. Power clean	4 x 5							
4. Pulldown behind neck	4 x 10							
5. Triceps (pushdowns–machine)	4 x 10							
6. Bentarm pullovers	4 x 10							
7. Dumbbell swings	4 x 10							
8. Hack squats	4 x 10							
9. Horizontal straight leg raisers	30 total							

Swim Gear

Diving
    Suit
    Warmups
    Sammy towel
    Diving flash cards

Competitive Swimming
    Swimsuit, cap, warmups
    Goggles
    Sammy towel
    Stopwatch

Synchronized Swimming
    Synchro suit
    Lycra or latex cap
    Nose clips
    Goggles

Water Polo
    Water polo suit and cap
    Ear guards
    Warmups
    Water polo ball

Open Water Swimming
    Swimsuit or wetsuit
    Insulated cap or 2 caps
    Goggles
    Vaseline
    Warm clothing for afterwards

Equipment to Improve Swim Technique

Zoomers

A minifin to enhance the kick

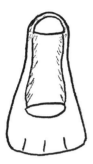

Snorkel

For body balance, body alignment and thoracic muscle strength

Paddles

To correct arm pull mechanics

Monofin

For speed, strength and just plain fun

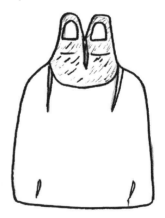

Hydro hip

For proper hip rotation

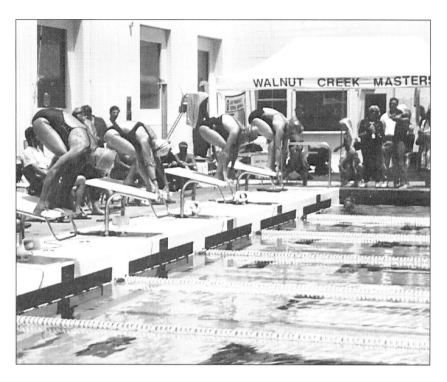

Above:

Racing start at Pacific Masters Champion-ship meet.

Left:

Snorkeling in warm waters.

From Near and Far

Members of Team Brazil at FINA International Meet,
Montreal, 1994

NOTES

NOTES

NOTES